Wild Flowe

D1448241

which you love an
enjoy

13.7. 85.

Sandy

Wild Flowers

In Their Habitat

Lord, to you we bring our treasure,
Wealth of mind & hand & heart,
Fruit of toil & joy & leisure,
Nature's world & craftsman's art.

Ackn. H. C. P. Gaunt

Desmond and Marjorie Parish

With Compliments & Best wishes

Desmond Parish

Marjorie Parish.

BLANDFORD PRESS
Poole   Dorset

Paperback edition first published in the U.K. 1984
by Blandford Press, Link House, West Street,
Poole, Dorset, BH15 1LL

Originally published in hardback 1979 as *Wild
Flowers – A Photographic Guide*

Copyright © 1979 and 1984 Blandford Press Ltd.

Distributed in the United States by
Sterling Publishing Co. Inc.,
2 Park Avenue, New York, N.Y. 10016

British Library Cataloguing in Publication Data

Parish, Desmond
    Wild flowers
        1. Wild Flowers – Pictorial works.
        I. Title   II, Parish, Marjorie.
        582′.13′0222   QK98

ISBN 0 7137 1395 X

Filmset by Keyspools Ltd., Golborne,
Lancashire.
Printed in Great Britain by W. S. Cowell Ltd.,
Ipswich, Suffolk.

Contents

To the memory of my Father

Introduction

Long before our arrival on this earth, its surface was covered with a living green mantle, the plants, primitive at first but slowly evolving into the species we see now. These have an extraordinary history of evolution and survival, their geographical range is enormous, and their physical adaptations to widely differing situations or habitats are astonishing in their variety. Their beauty of form and colour have been a joy and inspiration through centuries of time.

However, the most amazing fact is that of all living organisms, only plants are able to manufacture food products essential for their own existence, and equally necessary for that of the whole animal kingdom – including the human race. This they do by a wonderful process which combines the aid of sunlight with their own green colouring matter. We are all completely dependent upon this process and the vital importance of the plant-world cannot therefore be over-estimated.

We have taken much from the plants, including many useful things in addition to food, and we must continue to do so. Unfortunately, people have also greatly reduced the plants' living space for human purposes. Now enlightened persons realise that for all we take we must give something back. Therefore, the practice of wildlife conservation is spreading throughout the world, as evidenced by the provision of National Parks, Nature Reserves, Botanic Gardens and Wildfowl Sanctuaries. Most European countries accord some legal protection for wildlife and rare plants, including Great Britain (the Conservation of Wild Creatures and Wild Plants Act 1975). In fact, conservation organisations throughout the world are looking for support and practical help with their work.

This earth still has space for its abundant and marvellous life, but the responsibility of keeping the delicate balance for future generations now rests largely on the shoulders of mankind.

In this book we portray ninety-five of Europe's approximate number of seventeen thousand wild flowering-plants, a small sample of the riches we still possess. They range from the British Isles and the Arctic Circle to the shores of the Mediterranean Sea, from the Atlantic Coast to the border of Asia, and from sea-level to more than 4300 metres (14,000 feet) in altitude. Some present-day species have even survived the distant Ice Ages, through eons of time.

We have grouped the plants according to their habitats, giving a more natural pattern than any arrangement of colour or scientific classification, but this must be somewhat flexible. Although some species are very restricted in their type of situation, others overflow from one to another, for example, woodlands to roadsides, or even grow as far apart as high mountains and arctic regions.

Some plants are also variable in size and growth according to local conditions and climate; within our experience we have given an average range for each plant.

The scientific (Latin) names used are those of *Flora Europaea* (volumes 1 to 4) already published. For those plants not included until volume 5 is available, our references are *Flowers of Europe, Orchids of Britain and Europe* and *Flora of the British Isles*.

The English names follow those set down in *English Names of Wild Flowers*. A full Bibliography appears on page 162.

The subject of national names is a worthwhile study in itself, as most flowers in all countries have acquired a fascinating range of local names which can be only lightly introduced in a book of this kind.

Today, almost every household possesses one or more cameras, used to record family activities and hobbies. In this book the miracle of colour photography – and it is a miracle – has enabled us to reveal the beauty of wild flowers in their varied situations, a test of technique and artistic achievement.

The photographs were taken with an Exakta, the original single-lens reflex camera, using extension tubes for macro-shots with a 50 mm Zeiss Pancolar lens. As our photography was undertaken from early morning to late evening, and in all weather conditions, electronic flash was an essential accessory. This factor overcomes poor light conditions, eliminates wind movement and offers considerably better depth of focus. The camera lens is interchangeable with wide-angle and telephoto lenses for special applications. The film used was Kodachrome 25.

Desmond is the photographer and Marjorie the botanist, and on our botanical wanderings and in our presentations of illustrated slide-lectures and exhibitions of large format colour prints we have been privileged to meet many people of different nationalities, as well as our own, with similar interests. We have shared their companionship on mountains, in bogs and by the sea; we have enjoyed their generous hospitality and expert help and guidance in wild places. We have worked with them on committees devoted to conservation and natural history, and appreciated their queries and comments in lecture halls and museum galleries. Most of all we have benefited from their infectious enthusiasm, interest and encouragement. Thanks go especially to Mrs Anne Matterson, formerly Senior Botany Mistress at Queen Anne Grammar School, York, England, now of Ucluelet, Vancouver Island, Canada, for constant help and inspiration.

Indirectly, they have all helped with the making of this book and for them and others like them it has been produced.

Desmond and Marjorie Parish

Sea Pink, Thrift *Armeria maritima*
Family: Plumbaginaceae

Habitat and Distribution Maritime. On cliffs, sea walls, in saltmarshes and on stable shingle. Common around the coast of the British Isles and of Europe except the Eastern Mediterranean. Occasionally in mountains.

Flowering-time April to October.

Description The dancing heads of Sea Pink are probably the best known and best loved of all coastal flowers for they grow abundantly in almost every type of maritime situation. In May, thousands of beautiful pink 'buttons' make of the cliffs a rock-garden, of the saltmarsh a carpet. Our photograph shows a typical group perched above the encroaching waves, on rock encrusted with brilliant orange lichen, a most evocative picture of the long days of summer.

The plants are perennial with long, branching roots and grass-like leaves, and are very variable in size according to situation. One inflorescence consists of about 30 flowers, each with a tubular calyx and five pink petals interspersed with papery bracts. After flowering, these bracts are persistent and give the heads a characteristic straw-coloured appearance.

Points of Interest Thrift belongs to a group of plants found in large numbers by the sea and in smaller quantities in mountains. It is thought that this dual habitat has resulted from the disruption of the plants' once continuous distribution throughout Europe and the British Isles before their separation. During the Late Glacial Period as the ice melted, species which could not survive the competition of stronger colonising plants, retreated to open spaces.

1

Sea-kale *Crambe maritima*
Family: Cruciferae

Habitat Maritime. Prefers coastal shingle, especially along the driftline, just above high water mark. Sometimes on sandy beaches, rarely on cliffs.

Distribution In the British Isles it is uncommon and local, chiefly along the south coast of England and from North Wales to south-west Scotland and the Isle of Man. Very rare on the east coast and in Ireland. In Europe it is found on the north-west coast of Brittany to the Baltic Sea, also north-west Spain and shore of the Black Sea; local not common.

Flowering-time June to August.

Description These plants are large in every way, and obviously belong to the cabbage family. Their long-stalked leaves are a lovely shade of blue-green, very big, thick and glabrous, wavy at the edges, crimpled and curled and when young tinged with reddish-purple. Although found only locally, where they do grow they make in spring a beautiful design in soft colouring on the inhospitable pebbly ridge with little or no competition from other vegetation.

The big, white flowers are crowded in summer on long branching stems above the leaves, thus keeping the plants still conspicuously handsome, for they are then spreading widely in all directions and are about 60 cm (2 ft) tall. Each flower shows the typical Cruciferae structure, in this case 4 small green sepals which soon fall, 4 white petals, large and rounded, 4 long and 2 short stamens and a central pistil.

The seed-pods which follow are globular, up to 15 mm (nearly $\frac{3}{4}$ in) across, green at first becoming brown and hard so that the stalks present the appearance of having been threaded with a multitude of outsize beads.

Each pod contains one seed; dispersal is by sea-water in which the pods can float for several days while the seeds remain viable.

The plants are perennial each growing from a stout rootstock. In their exposed position they are constantly in danger of burial or uprooting through disturbance of the loose stones of their habitat. However, they are well adapted to counter these risks because the thick rootstock can produce horizontal underground shoots when necessary to keep them firmly anchored.

Point of Interest As with many members of Cruciferae, Sea-kale is edible, and one reason for its scarce distribution now, at least in Britain, is that it used to be gathered extensively for its food value and was also transplanted from the wild into gardens. The leaf-stalks are considered a great delicacy and are cut when the leaves are just developing. Under cultivation they are first blanched by the exclusion of light, and for the table are boiled and eaten like asparagus.

As it is now easy to grow the plants from cultivated stock or seed the few remaining wild reserves of this interesting plant should be left alone to play their part in beautifying and helping to stabilise the bleak but fascinating shingle beaches where they grow.

Yellow Horned-poppy *Glaucium flavum*
Family: Papaveraceae

Habitat Maritime. Locally common on coastal shingle, occasionally on sand and sea cliffs, rarely a short distance inland on chalk or limestone.

Distribution In the British Isles, from south-west Scotland on the west coast, and from the Wash on the east, southwards, and throughout the south coast of England in suitable places. Less common in Ireland, mostly on the eastern side, but found throughout Europe in similar situations on all coasts from Greece in the Mediterranean northwards to Sweden.

Flowering-time June to September, earlier on Mediterranean beaches.

Description Scattered around the coasts of Britain and Europe are these very lovely plants of the shingle beaches, which are gay in summer with their big golden-yellow flowers. The whole plant, usually large and spreading and up to 90 cm (3 ft) tall, is glaucous green with that succulent texture characteristic of many maritime species but not found in other European poppies. The stems are sturdy and the rather coarsely-cut leaves thick and tough, but the beautiful petals, four as usual in this family, are of that delicate softness which poppies always produce. The two large green sepals covered with short thick hairs, part slowly to reveal these yellow petals, so finely crinkled at first, and then, as the flower opens to its full extent of some 5 cm (2 in) the petals smoothen and the sepals fall, their work of protection being over.

Following the flowers are the fruits, the peculiar hallmark of this genus; curved green pods from 15–30 cm (6–12 in) long and the origin of the plant's English name 'horned'. These pods give the plants a shaggy appearance in autumn as they turn yellowish-brown and split lengthwise into two halves, thus exposing the numerous seeds for dispersal over the shingle.

The plants are usually biennial with a long taproot and the rosettes of new crinkled leaves can be seen in spring, flat to the beach, and in themselves a most attractive harbinger of the beauty that is to come.

Points of Interest The seed-head of most members of Papavaraceae is a flask-shaped capsule covered by a cap at the top, and with a ring of holes beneath the cap from which the small hard seeds are blown as the stems sway in the wind. The genus *Glaucium* (2 species in Europe, the other being *G. corniculatum* with red flowers) and *Roemera hybrida* with violet flowers, are markedly different from other European poppies in the production of the long curved pods as here described.

Golden Samphire *Inula crithmoides*
Family: Compositae

Habitat Maritime; rocky cliffs to high water mark; less frequently shingle and saltmarshes.
Distribution Local on south-west coasts of Europe and British Isles (England and Wales).
Flowering-time July to October.
Description The haunts of Golden Samphire are exciting, especially when flowering-time coincides with autumnal gales which lash high seas against fierce jagged rocks where it abounds. Plants of bright yellow-green are readily distinguishable from the typical blue-grey-green maritime vegetation as the sun-rayed flowerheads embellish spray-washed cliffs with gold.

The necessary anchorage of a long woody rootstock produces clusters of smooth stems, usually from 15 to 30 cm (6 to 12 in) tall, and clothed with narrow fleshy sessile leaves. The brilliant inflorescences display an inner disc of tubular florets, more orange than the outer spreading rays which attract pollinating insects. Numerous feathery seeds are produced, easily whisked away by strong coastal breezes, to lodge in crevices suitable for germination.

Points of Interest Three maritime plants are named 'Samphire', the others being Rock Samphire *Crithmum maritimum* (Umbelliferae) and Marsh Samphire *Salicornia europaea* (Chenopodiaceae). Botanically this is misleading, but there is a captivating explanation. 'Samphire' is reputedly an English contraction of the French *Saint Pierre* – Saint Peter to whom Christ entrusted the keys of the Kingdom of Heaven. The leaves of all 3 plants are similar, resembling the saint's precious bundle of keys.

Sea Bindweed *Calystegia soldanella*
Family: Convolvulaceae

Habitat Maritime. Open sand-dunes, occasionally shingle.
Distribution In Britain, local, chiefly England, Wales. In Europe, the Atlantic and Mediterranean coasts from Denmark southwards; east to Russia.
Flowering-time May to September.
Description Can there be any more fascinating coastal plants than these? Their large shell-pink and white trumpets lying on pure sand, sometimes with no visible means of support, form a glorious picture long to be remembered when the sea is left behind. The smooth reddish stems cannot grow upright but possess great strength in pushing through the wind-blown sand of the dunes and beaches. Even though temporarily buried, as often they are, the plants survive and the delicate flowers and kidney-shaped dark green leathery leaves are soon above ground again. The buds are beautiful with 2 reddish-green bracts surrounding the calyx; the newly opening flowers resemble tightly folded little parasols before they gradually unfurl into the tubular wide trumpets 3 to 5 cm (up to 2 in) long as seen in the photograph.
Points of Interest The Italian word *soldo* meaning 'a coin' is the basis for this plant's specific name and an interesting link with the alpine genus *Soldanella*. All these possess similar leaves, rounded and glossy like a small coin, which are able to reject surplus water whether from sea-spray or melting snow as well as preventing excess evaporation of water from within the plants by drying winds.

7

Round-leaved Wintergreen *Pyrola rotundifolia* subsp. *maritima*
Family: Pyrolaceae

Habitat Damp places in pinewoods, wet mountain ledges, bogs (the type plant), wet slacks in coastal sand-dunes (subsp. maritima).

Distribution Rare and thinly scattered in Britain, mostly in the Scottish Highlands, and sand-dunes of Wales and West coast of England. However, it is widely scattered, but not common, through most of Europe, more especially in northern areas, and on the Atlantic coast from north-west France to West Germany.

Flowering-time June to September depending on latitude and altitude.

Description The pale drooping flowers of the Pyrolas may occasionally be found in summer beneath the cool shade of coniferous woods, mostly in hills and mountains, where their comparatively small numbers provide a quietly beautiful picture of green and white in damp mossy ground or on wet ferny ledges. By contrast they flower in glorious abundance amidst the silver-grey carpets of creeping willow, *Salix repens* in northern sand-dune slacks. These are freshwater hollows between the dry sand-hills which produce a wonderful wealth of plants, the Pyrolas being amongst the most beautiful of them.

These plants of such delicate appearance are perennials with a slender creeping rootstock from which arises a circlet of rounded leaves $2\frac{1}{2}$–4 cm (1–$1\frac{1}{2}$ in) long on stalks just a little longer. The leaf-blades are dark glossily green, slightly indented and persistent through the winter, hence the name wintergreen. The flowers are borne on reddish stems up to 20 cm (8 in) tall, erect and unbranched, on which are a few small leaflike scales. From 8 to 14 pure white pendent flowers form a loose raceme some 6 cm ($2\frac{1}{4}$ in) in length. Each flower consists of 5 green sepals, 5 rounded spreading petals, 5 stamens with orange anthers and a distinctive protruding curved pink style ending in a blunt stigma. The style is a distinguishing point between the several species of Pyrola.

Points of Interest Two forms of *Pyrola rotundifolia* grow in two widely differing but damp habitats as already indicated. The differences between the plants are small; we have illustrated and described a dune plant *P. rotundifolia* subsp. *maritima*. Its arrival in the dunes is comparatively recent (1855 in Britain) and both that and its expanding development are of extremely great interest. It is probable that the plants came originally with the introduction of pine planting on the dunes by the Forestry Commission, and the rich humus provided by the decay of the willow (*Salix repens*) has enabled them to spread.

This form is endemic to north-west Europe, but *P. rotundifolia* is widely distributed in the northern hemisphere from North America across Europe into central and northern Asia.

The aromatic Oil of Wintergreen used for the relief of rheumatism has *no* connection with these plants but is extracted from a species of *Gaultheria*, a native of North America, whose leaves are also evergreen.

Scottish Primrose *Primula scotica*
Family: Primulaceae

Habitat Short coastal turf on cliff grassland.
Distribution Endemic to Scotland. Occasional on the north coast and on the Orkney Islands, on Durness limestone.
Flowering-time Between June and September.
Description This is one of the gems of the British flora. On the rugged cliffs of Scotland's northern coast, subject to wild winds, stormy showers and outbursts of brilliant sunshine even during the flowering-season, the small plants nestle snugly amongst other vegetation, itself rich in colour and variety. It is a tremendous thrill to stand here surrounded by a glorious profusion of Scottish bluebells (*Campanula rotundifolia*), wild orchids, scabious, vetches, yellow bedstraw – and much more – and look out across the wind-caught breakers to the horizon, no land at all between you and the North Pole, nearly 2200 miles away. At your feet is the marvellous contrast of the small brilliant flowers of the Scottish primrose glowing vividly in the almost day-long hours of light through the short northern summer.

The flower-stalks, scarcely 5 cm (2 in) tall, grow from a leafy rosette lying close to the turf; the leaves are green and wrinkled above, mealy and greyish beneath. From about 4 to 8 flowers are produced in an umbel, upright and with 5 spreading petals of a rich and rare shade of red-purple with yellow centres. The flowers differ from the more familiar wild primulas in that the 5 stamens and single pistil are always at the same depth within the flower-tube. Typical primroses produce 2 flower-forms, 'pin-eyed' where the pistil is visible at the throat, with the stamens hidden below, and 'thrum-eyed' where the reverse is the case. This arrangement normally ensures cross-pollination by insects, but *P. scotica* is more dependent upon self-fertilisation because of the relative scarcity of insects where it grows.

Points of Interest Through the passage of time species of plants, animals – and man! – have developed, and still are developing according to their situation. Where some major natural cause (for example, the flooding of the Mediterranean basin, and the covering of the Arctic ice-caps) has separated groups of like species these have often evolved in different ways. As each is native to, and found wild only in one restricted area, they are said to be endemic to that area. The Mediterranean islands are all rich in endemic plants; the British Isles unfortunately are poor, *P. scotica* being one of the most interesting and beautiful. It is related to *P. farinosa* a bigger plant with lilac flowers, widespread in the northern hemisphere, and from which species it is probable that *P. scotica* and similar rare primulas endemic to Scandinavia have developed.

It is extremely important that the heritage of these scarce endemic plants should be protected in their native countries and held in trust by them for the benefit of the world as a whole. If ever they become extinct they are unlikely ever to return.

French Lavender *Lavandula stoechas*
Family: Labiatae

Habitat Mediterranean Europe (except Yugoslavia and Albania) and Portugal. On siliceous soil.

Distribution Locally common on dry stony hillsides of the maquis and garigue, occasionally penetrating some miles inland.

Flowering-time April to June; earlier in the eastern Mediterranean.

Description Where French lavender grows on the dry sunny slopes above the Mediterranean coastline we are rewarded with a picture of memorable beauty. The plants are unmistakable with their rich-purple 'topknots' waving above grey-violet flowering spikes, which themselves thrust up beyond the grey-green leafy twigs. Mingled as they frequently are with pink and white cistus blossoms, they present a wonderful pageant of colour, especially when backed by the blue of the sea and sky and the glowing red of the volcanic porphyry rocks of the Esterel on the Côte d'Azur.

The shrubs attain a height of about 60 cm (2 ft) with tough woody stems, the upper ones thickly clothed with narrow pointed leaves. These vary from 6–20 mm ($\frac{1}{4}$–2 in) long with inrolled margins and are grey-green due to the covering of fine hairs, a characteristic frequently encountered in plants of dry situations.

The true flowers grow in four-sided spikes 2–3 cm ($1\frac{3}{4}$–$2\frac{1}{4}$ in) long, where they are subtended by greyish hairy bracts. The flowers are very small, dark purple, almost velvety in appearance, and as they open at varying times the spike is irregularly patterned with their starry shapes. These are the seed-producing flowers; the conspicuous and colourful tufts above them each consist of four uneven long bracts which attract pollinating insects. Nature has many ways of providing flowers with the power of insect-attraction and surely this is one of the most peculiarly beautiful.

The plant in our photograph shows an unusual variation of the typical purple colour; there the tufted bracts are pink with darker veining, and the true flowers are rich magenta.

Points of Interest This species is aromatic like the cultivated lavender *Lavandula angustifolia* familiar in gardens, but the oil extracted from it is less valuable. Sprigs of it are used for perfuming linen and as a moth-deterrent in southern Europe as are those of *L. angustifolia* in Britain. *L. angustifolia* is a native of sunny inland hills and Provence in France has become the world's centre of the perfume industry as a result of its wealth of this and other aromatic plants. The industry has now expanded tremendously through local commercial cultivation and also large-scale importation of worldwide exotic species.

Bladder Senna *Colutea arborescens*
Family: Leguminosae.

Habitat Woods and bushy places on limestone hills; sometimes naturalised on waste ground.

Distribution Not native to Britain, but introduced as an ornamental shrub in the sixteenth century, now naturalised occasionally on railway banks and waste places. In Europe it is native, circum Mediterranean, including North Africa, south-east and central Europe, spreading into western Asia.

Flowering-time April to July.

Description On the grey limestone hills behind the Mediterranean coast we can find this peculiarly handsome, thornless shrub amongst the numerous spiny species typical of these sunny slopes. They grow erect to a height of about 4 m (13 ft) and their attractive pinnate leaves provide a welcome touch of fresh light green as contrast to the greyish shade which is here so predominent. Each leaf is divided into 7 to 15 oval leaflets, rather smooth and from 5–15 mm ($\frac{1}{4}$ to $\frac{3}{4}$ in) long.

The pale yellow flowers, lightly marked with red, are borne in pendulous clusters on short erect stalks, and display the typical floral structure of the leguminous family. The 5 petals are uneven in shape and size, and consist of a large rounded notched 'standard', 2 side 'wings' and a central horizontal 'keel' made up of 2 petals folded together into a tube surrounding 10 stamens and the pistil. Because of this unusually charming arrangement of the petals they are described as papilionaceous ('butterfly') flowers and seen at their best in our cultivated sweet pea of the same family.

The most noteworthy parts of *Colutea* are the seed-pods, which resemble papery balloons, reddish-brown, and quite large, about 4 to 7 cm ($1\frac{1}{2}$ to $2\frac{3}{4}$ in) long and half as wide. They are smooth and shining with an upturned pointed tip. These inflated pods enable the plants to be distinguished easily from the many yellow-flowered leguminous shrubs which fling such a wonderful blaze of gold over the Mediterranean cliffs and hinterland in springtime.

Point of Interest The name Senna gives a clue to the past use of this plant. True senna is obtained from plants of the genus *Cassia* which are mostly tropical and closely related to Leguminosae. The leaves and seeds of *Colutea arborescens* like the leaves of the *Cassias* are purgative and have been used as a substitute for the original senna. They are poisonous to cattle.

Nicholas Culpeper, the English herbalist, writing of this plant in his *Complete Herbal*, published in 1653, says very simply 'The common Bladder Senna (*Colutea arborescens*) works very violently both upwards and downwards', which should act as fair warning to any would-be experimenters!

Wild Gladiolus *Gladiolus illyricus*
Family: Iridaceae

Habitat Grassy and bushy places, damp fields.

Distribution Found only in the New Forest in Britain and very rare. Protected by law. Elsewhere in Europe, found in Portugal and Mediterranean coasts except Turkey. Also North Balkans and northern Austria.

Flowering-time April to July.

Description Each year, springtime colours the shores and hillsides around the Mediterranean with a brilliant display of flowers second to none in Europe. Amongst them the soldierly spikes of wild gladioli convert meadows and fields into quilts of glowing carmine as myriads of flowers bloom atop the grasses and shorter plants. Amongst thorny bushes and scrub of the dry hill-slopes they are seen again but in small scattered groups which splash patches of the same warm glow across the typical green-grey background. Our photograph depicts one of the several similar species which flaunt this beauty so vividly, a small graceful form and the only one with a foothold as far north as England. There it grows, very sparingly indeed by Mediterranean standards, in the mild climate of the hinterland of the south coast, its rosy flowers richly beautiful amongst the bright fresh green of bracken.

Each plant develops from a corm 15 mm (about $\frac{1}{2}$ in) in diameter, a solid rounded underground stem and a food store through the winter. From this corm a slender stem reaches a height of 30 to 60 cm (1 to 2 ft), sheathed with a few shorter leaves, narrow and stiffly-pointed. The stem produces a rather loose spike of from 3 to 8 large carmine-red flowers each subtended by two uneven shorter purplish bracts. The flowers are composed of 6 coloured petal-like segments, the upper one longer and broader than the others, the three lowest being the narrowest. These 3 are delicately enhanced with pale yellow stripes outlined with purple. Within the petals are 3 stamens with yellow anthers shorter than their stalks (a point to be watched when identifying gladiolus species) and a long slender style divided into 3 stigmas. Later the seeds are enclosed in a round green capsule, about 5 mm (0.25 in) diameter.

Points of Interest The name is taken from the Latin *gladius*, meaning a sword, because of the sharp pointed leaves; the plants are sometimes called Sword-lilies. As a native of the warm sunny Mediterranean area it is remarkable that this lovely gladiolus should also be found in Great Britain, and understandable that its distribution there has always been severely restricted to the milder south. But it has now become extinct in many of its former stations; its stately beauty and vivid colouring have made it an obvious target for flower-pickers, and its need for protection from them is now very great indeed. That is why it is included in the U.K. Conservation of Wild Creatures and Wild Plants Act as a completely protected plant (see page vii). The plants are still at risk because of their situation in a popular holiday area and it cannot be emphasised too strongly that they must not be picked or damaged at all. Such malpractice incurs a heavy legal penalty. If left alone they may eventually increase in numbers to delight those who are fortunate enough to see and appreciate their beauty.

Bertoloni's Bee Orchid *Ophrys bertolonii*
Family: Orchidaceae

Habitat Mediterranean. Stony grassy places, open clearings and margins of pinewoods.
Distribution Most of Mediterranean Europe from Spain to Yugoslavia and Bulgaria. Rather rare.
Flowering-time March to June.
Description Orchids, more than any other plants, exert a mysterious fascination for most people, and of all the wild orchids of Europe, the genus *Ophrys* is the most puzzling and peculiar. The flowers of *Ophrys* always resemble insects, but with so many variations on the theme that correct identification is difficult, and often impossible for the beginner. Thus, our choice of *Ophrys bertolonii* to represent the genus, though partly because of its beauty, is also because it is one of the least variable members. Small groups or colonies may sometimes be seen in grassy clearings amongst shrubby vegetation, when the sudden sight of a number of these enchanting little plants is a wonderful reward for a thorny scratchy search. Their exotic purple-brown velvety flowers are in such marked contrast to the large simple but spectacular rock-roses (*Cistus*) often surrounding them.

The plants vary from 10 to 30 cm (4 to 12 in) tall, with 5 or 6 basal light green leaves and 1 or 2 smaller stem-leaves. From 2 to 6 flowers open from the lowest upwards; of the 6 petal-like parts one forms a large hanging lip with the remaining 5 spread out above it. Three wider pink or purple (rarely green) ones alternate with 2 narrow ones of a darker shade and all marked with a prominent green vein. The lip is the most peculiar and the distinguishing mark of this genus. That of *Ophrys bertolonii* is long, 15 to 20 mm (to $\frac{3}{4}$in) with a rather square end; the upper half is dark brown and softly hairy, while across the lower half shines a patch of luminous blue which fades as the flower grows older. At the base of the lip is a small but distinctive green outward-pointing appendage.

The stamens and pistils of orchids are different from those of other plants and in our lower flower can be seen the 2 yellow pollinia, which replace the normal separate stamens.
Points of Interest Orchids are plants which merit special protection wherever they grow and in whatever quantity; fortunately many are now protected by law in several countries including *Ophrys bertolonii*. They are extremely slow-growing, even the simplest forms taking several years to produce their first flowers. If these are picked the underground tubers can be damaged irreparably and the plants lost for ever, and of course neither can seed be set. As all European species are comparatively rare – (that is, not found commonly throughout the continent) and many are very scarce indeed, the hard rule should be – *never* pick or damage even one orchid plant.

Ploughshare Orchid *Serapias vomeracea*
Family: Orchidaceae

Habitat Mediterranean region. Scrub, damp grassy and sandy places from sea-level to 900 m (3000 ft).

Distribution Circum Mediterranean, Portugal, Bulgaria. Also Switzerland (very rare and protected in the southern part).

Flowering-time April to June.

Description The dark wine or brick-red flowers of the genus *Serapias* belong only to the Mediterranean region of the world and are easily distinguishable from all other European orchids. About 16 to 23 cm (6 to 9 in) tall, they grow usually in small groups amongst damp grass and are readily seen against the contrasting background of bright green. There is nothing strange or bizarre about them, as with the *Ophrys* species, but they diffuse a slight air of mystery, perhaps because of their unusual form, their muted colour range, and their restricted world distribution. The last fact alone provides a tremendous thrill for any non-Mediterranean botanist on his first meeting with them.

This is one of 6 species very similar in form, structure and colouring but because of hybridisation within the genus and with other orchid species, correct identification can be confusing. Stems and leaves are smooth, and green below, the stems sometimes tinged purple above. The flowering-spike rises above the leaves and consists of from 3 to 8 fairly large flowers suffused with purplish-red. The large lower petal characteristic of orchids, known as the lip or labellum, is the main distinguishing point of the genus, being long, pointed and pendant, and giving the name 'Tongue Orchid' to this group. It has 2 sections the upper being a spreading platform at least partly hidden by the remaining 5 silvery-red petals which are fused into a surrounding hood. The lower section of the lip, the 'tongue', is in *S. vomeracea*, very long $2\frac{1}{2}$–3 cm (1–$1\frac{1}{4}$ in) and narrows gradually to a sharp point. Because of its supposed resemblance to the shape of a ploughshare (the cutting blade of the plough) this species is sometimes given the name Ploughshare Orchid and the specific name *vomeracea* also refers to that point. Each flower grows in the axil of a bract, in this species longer than the flower and of a softer purple colour than the dark reddish lip. Bracts, petals and lip are all delicately marked with darker red veining.

Points of Interest This is the only member of the genus *Serapias* found as far away from the Mediterranean as Switzerland, where it is rare in a few southern valleys and is strongly protected there.

The name *Serapias* honours Serapis the principal deity once worshipped in the Greek and Roman towns of Egypt, his temple in Alexandria being the last stronghold of the pagans after the introduction of Christianity to that country.

Grey-leaved Rockrose *Cistus albidus*
Family: Cistaceae

Habitat Mediterranean. Coastal garigue, stony ground, especially limestone.
Distribution Portugal, Spain, Balearic Islands, France, Italy. Often abundant. Not British.
Flowering-time April to June.
Description The beauty of the Mediterranean Rockroses lies in countless numbers of large simple flowers wide open through long days of warm sunshine, and in the remarkable succession of these ephemeral pink and white blossoms. Each lives but a day, yet they follow one another in tremendous profusion.

Cistus albidus is a pink-flowered species of western distribution, to 90 cm (3 ft) tall, forming dense thickets amongst which many unusual herbaceous plants find shelter. The velvety leaves, whitish-grey with hairs, grow in crowded stalkless pairs. In spring they are almost hidden by the flowers, 4 to 6 cm (to $2\frac{1}{2}$ in) across, gorgeously pink, softly crinkled and with a rich golden pack of stamens in the centre.

Points of Interest *Cistus* shrubs are aromatic, the most useful being the similar pink-flowered *C. incanus* and *C. ladanifer* whose white flowers are adorned with chocolate blotches. Both possess fragrant sticky leaves and young shoots from which laudanum is obtained, in olden times by scraping the gum from the plants and combing the fleeces of grazing animals and even the beards of goats. Now the shoots are cut and dissolved in alcohol to extract the laudanum, still used in perfumery and the preparation of some medical dressings.

Large-Flowered Orlaya *Orlaya grandiflora*
Family: Umbelliferae

Habitat Roadsides, waste ground, especially on limestone and clay.
Distribution Mediterranean, central and south-east Europe. Not British.
Flowering-time Between May and September depending upon situation.
Description The umbrella-like flower-heads of the Umbelliferae family provide one of the most familiar sights of the European summer flora for they flourish exceedingly along country roadsides and in uncultivated grassland. Typical frothy white masses of inflorescences are massed in circular clusters above a fernlike array of deeply-cut leaves.

Orlaya grandiflora is easily identified when flowering by the large outer petals which are from 5 to 8 times the size of the extremely tiny central ones. The plants may reach 50 cm (20 in) tall with ridged branching stems and very finely divided leaves, the upper sessile, the lower stalked. Each inflorescence has 5 to 10 rays or 'spokes' with it own tight head of small perfect florets, the whole surrounded by the conspicuous 2-lobed petals.

Points of Interest Several umbelliferous plants possess unevenly sized petals including the almost ubiquitous Hogweed *Heracleum sphondylium*, but the difference in size is far more marked in *O. grandiflora* than in any other. That arrangement and the crowding of numerous small florets into one large inflorescence combine to make the plants attractive to insects and ensure cross-pollination. The seeds are small and hard and in this plant (*Orlaya*) are clothed with long bristly white hairs.

Woad *Isatis tinctoria*
Family: Cruciferae

Habitat Roadsides, waste places, usually a relic of cultivation.
Distribution Naturalised in England, once fairly widespread, but now very rare. Widespread but local throughout Europe except Iceland.
Flowering-time May to August.
Description The Cruciferae family includes a number of tall leafy yellow-flowered plants not always easy to distinguish from one another. Woad is one of the most attractive of these which spreads large many-flowered panicles in bright golden profusion along roadside verges and in grassy waste ground in summer. This picture, however, applies only to Europe where the plants are much more numerous than in England.

The plants are usually biennial with tall erect much-branched stems from 90–120 cm (3–4 ft) high, and with slightly glaucous leaves, the upper ones clasping the stem with ear-shaped points. The lower leaves are stalked, 5–10 cm (2–4 in) long, slightly indented and oval-oblong in shape.

The flowers are individually very small, less than 6 mm ($\frac{1}{4}$ in) across, but so prolific and crowded on the upper branches that they produce a bright waving foam of colour above the surrounding vegetation. Each flower has 4 tiny sepals, 4 petals (typical of Cruciferae) and 6 stamens, 4 long and 2 short ones. After flowering the flower-stalks lengthen and curl over, the seed-pods grow to about 18 mm ($\frac{3}{4}$ in) long, dry and pale brown with a prominent flattened wing at each side of the single hard seed. At this stage they present an unusual appearance of numerous hanging bunches of small keys, making recognition of the plant easy.

Points of Interest The outstanding interest of this quite attractive plant is its use as a source of rich blue-purple dye, which was obtained from the leaves by grinding them to a paste, and allowing that to ferment. Its use has been known from at least 1000 B.C. by which time it was in cultivation in Northern Europe. It was later introduced into Britain more than 1000 years ago, and its use was continued until the early part of this century, since when synthetic dyes have superseded it.

Its fame in history is its use by the 'Ancient Britons' to paint their bodies for battle (or perhaps adornment). Later it became one of the standard dyes for cloth and was much cultivated for that purpose. It was frequently mixed with the yellow dyes obtained from the wild plants *Genista tinctoria* (Dyer's Greenweed) and *Reseda luteola* (Dyer's Rocket or Weld) to produce the well-known colours of Kendal and Lincoln green, the latter helping to clothe Robin Hood and his Merry Men.

Common Poppy *Papaver rhoeas*
Family: Papaveraceae

Habitat Cultivated fields, especially associated with corn, waste places, roadsides, coastal shingle.

Distribution Widespread in the British Isles, but least common in northern Scotland and western Ireland. Found throughout Europe, except Iceland and Turkey. Uncommon in the north. Once frequent everywhere, but now much less so, due to the improved screening of seeds of food-crops, and better farming methods.

Flowering-time Between April and September.

Description A cornfield in summer dominated by the brilliant scarlet of poppies is now a comparatively rare sight but one which nevertheless still spells beauty for the onlooker, though far from pleasing to the farmer. The flowers are borne singly on erect branched stems growing up to 60 cm (2 ft) tall and leafy, especially in the lower half. The leaves are deeply divided into lobed sections and they and the stems are bristly with short outspreading hairs. So are the 2 green sepals which cover and protect the petals in bud, but which fall quickly as these petals gradually unfold, beautifully crumpled at first, then becoming smooth and silky as they reach their full size of 4–6 cm ($1\frac{1}{2}$–$2\frac{1}{4}$ in). The 2 outer larger ones overlap the 2 inner ones and all are frequently blotched darkly at the centre, where rings of black-anthered stamens surround the pistil. This is crowned with 8 to 12 dark ridges which are the stigmas and it later becomes the typical poppy seed-head, a cup – shaped capsule, which sheds its many small dry seeds from holes beneath the top (see *Glaucium flavum* on page 5).

It is due to the ability of these seeds to lie dormant for several years and then germinate in almost any type of disturbed soil that the plants appear so prolifically on arable land, and that in these times of constant disturbance of ground for such things as roadworks and buildings we find them so quickly splashing with their flaunting brilliance the ugly scars made by man's machinery. It is also due to this fact that the British poet John McRae gave to Europe his poignant and memorable poem of World War I:

> 'If ye break faith with us who die
> We shall not sleep, though poppies grow
> In Flanders fields.'

Let us be glad of the poppies and their abundant gift of swift vivid colonisation of bleak bare ground, sometimes in company with other so-called weeds of colourful contrast.

Points of Interest The specific name *rhoeas* is from the Greek for pomegranate, as the poppy capsules are supposed to have a superficial resemblance to that fruit, though much smaller.

The genus *Papaver* is well-known for its narcotic properties and infusions from the capsules of *P. rhoeas* were once used as a sedative. The much larger *P. somniferum* has long been cultivated as the source of the drug opium and is occasionally found as an escape. The large flowers vary from white to lilac in colour, with or without dark blotches.

Teasel *Dipsacus fullonum*
Family: Dipsacaceae

Habitat Roadsides, stream banks, open woods, waste places.

Distribution Widespread in the south-eastern half of England, less common northwards to south-east Scotland. Sparingly around the coast of Ireland. Found in most of Europe, except mountains and the far north.

Flowering-time July to September.

Description The tall, stiffly-branching plants of teasel cannot be mistaken or missed as they stand high above the surrounding vegetation, for their bristle-edged conical flower-heads are quite unlike those of any other plant of the European flora. They are peculiar in that the numerous small flowers encircle the cone with rings of purple giving a softly broken appearance to the already strange spiny spike. Backed by the sea or sky they have an air of having escaped from some distant desert to the lush green of Europe's riverbanks and roadsides.

The plants are biennial with, typically, a taproot topped by a ground-hugging rosette of leaves, long, crinkled, with scattered prickles on the upper surface and which wither (before flowering time) during the plants' second season. The erect branching stems are also prickly and from 60 to 180 cm (2 to 6 ft) tall. The stem-leaves grow in alternate pairs, clasping the stem at their joint bases to form a cup-like container in which rain-water is held. These leaves are long, ribbed and pointed, and spiny only on the underside of the broad midrib.

The flower-spikes, 5–8 cm (up to 3 in) long and 5 cm (2 in) wide, are held singly and erect on each branch but not all in bloom at the same time. The purple flowers are individually very small, about 4 mm (less than $\frac{1}{4}$ in) across with 4 petals formed into a narrow tube which is hidden amongst densely-packed short bracts, each of which terminates in a short spine. About 10 to 16 much longer bracts grow from the base of the cone, most of them exceeding its length, and these are shortly prickled along their edges. After the flowers die the spikes turn brown and remain on the old plants through the winter.

Points of Interest The plant is only slightly different from *D. sativus*, or Fuller's Teasel, but that difference was very important in the past. In that species the short bracts of the flower-head end in spines which are stiff and hooked and this is the plant which was used for 'teasing' or raising the nap of woollen cloth to give it a good surface. This is now done by machinery. Originally the prickly flower-cones were fixed round the circumference of a large wheel so that the hooked bristles could tease out the cloth as it was held firm against the moving wheel. *D. sativus* was widely cultivated for that purpose and naturalised plants (escapes from cultivation) are still occasionally found. Amongst the many local names given to the teasel two amusing ones are Venus's Bath in England and Cabaret des Oiseaux in France, both in reference to the retention of water by the large stem-clasping leaves.

Musk Mallow *Malva moschata*
Family: Malvaceae

Habitat Roadsides, dry banks, grassy places.

Distribution Widespread in southern half of England, occasional elsewhere in Britain. In most of the continent, widespread, local.

Flowering-time June to September, depending on latitude.

Description Musk Mallow is one of the most attractive roadside plants. Its beautiful pale rose-pink flowers are so large and neatly massed together at the ends of the hairy stalks that even from a distance one has the impression of delicate colouring combined with almost exotic loveliness. Closer examination reveals also the charming tracery of the light green leaves. There is no other hedgerow plant quite like it in form and colouring; its own relatives of the roadside verges, the common and creeping mallows, have flowers of a much more reddish-purple and a rather straggling habit.

The average height of the perennial Musk Mallow is about 60 cm (2 ft) and its branching habit gives the plants a somewhat bushy appearance especially as they are leafy and floriferous. The long-stalked leaves are rounded in outline, from 5 to 8 cm (2 to 3 in) across and palmately divided. The lower ones are lobed, sometimes only slightly, and the upper ones deeply cut into numerous narrow fingerlike segments, but all this is an extremely variable factor. When crushed the leaves produce a slight odour of musk, hence the specific name *moschata.*

The flowers, usually pale pink, occasionally white, are large, 5 cm (2 in) across, with 5 spreading petals, slightly notched and veined with darker pink. There are two rings of sepals, the outer comprising 3 small segments, and the inner 5 larger ones. In the centre of the flower is a peculiar column, formed by the fusion of the stalks of the stamens which are numerous. The anthers appear in a cluster at the top covered with yellow pollen when ripe. After this has been collected by insects the anthers shrivel and their place is taken by the stigmas, pushed up through the top of the hollow column by the style and ready to receive pollen from a different flower. Thus cross-pollination is effected, displaying another of nature's unusual ways of working.

Points of Interest The family Malvaceae is widespread throughout the world, and includes the well-known garden Hollyhocks, the exotic *Hibiscus* species, and the plant which gives us cotton, *Gossypium herbaceum*. *Malva moschata* is one of several plants supposed to have the scent of musk, in this case through the leaves. The original musk is a secretion from the male musk deer, a native of the mountains of central Asia, and it is collected for use in medicine and perfumery.

Meadow Clary *Salvia pratensis*
Family: Labiatae

Habitat Roadsides, dry grassland, pastures, on limestone.

Distribution In Britain, rare in a few localities in southern England. Widespread in central and southern Europe, introduced further north. Reaches 1920 m (6000 ft) in the mountains, though uncommon in the Pyrenees.

Flowering-time Between May and August.

Description One of the glories of subalpine pastures and roadsides, the vivid purple-blue Meadow Clary may dominate the local scene with an almost unbelievable brilliance of colour. As the large flowers grow in close whorls on tall leafless spikes the blue is almost unmixed with any other shade and even from a distance the picture is one to be long remembered. In the British Isles, however, these spikes occur in such scarcity as to make each individual one a special feature of beauty in itself, to be carefully treasured.

It would seem that the species likes a reasonably mild climate as its native distribution, both continental and British, is confined to warmer southern areas.

The sturdy plants are perennial, hairy, slightly aromatic, and grow to a height of from 30 to 60 cm (1 to 2 ft) so that a good colony can crowd out lesser vegetation to become dominant or can mix readily with other colourful meadow plants of similar height. The stems are square, as usual in Labiatae, with a few pairs of sessile dark green wrinkled leaves, similar to, but smaller than those of the basal rosette, which are from 7 to 13 cm (3 to 5 ins) long with stalks, and all have coarsely-toothed edges.

Flowers of this family are irregular in shape; their 5 petals are united into a tube which divides at the top into 2 distinct parts, an upper arching hood and a lower projecting lip, both easily identified in *Salvia pratensis*. The hood protects 2 stamens which are arched forward, as is the style whose 2 stigmas project well beyond the hood when ripe.

Points of Interest Nectar is secreted at the base of the flower-tube. To reach it a bee alights on the lower lip, pushes its head into the flower, and its proboscis down the tube. This action brings it into contact with a remarkable lever-mechanism possessed by the stamens and by which the anthers are brought down onto the bee's head and there deposit their pollen. If the bee then visits an older flower, the pollen is brushed off its body onto the ripe outstretched stigmas which are here in the correct position to receive it. Here is another wonderful method of cross-pollination.

The culinary herb of our kitchens is *Salvia officinalis* which scents the Mediterranean air with aromatic fragrance. Its blue flowers are paler than those of *S. pratensis* but its soft 'sage green' leaves are the basis also of a favourite country drink and a fine tonic. The name *Salvia* is of Latin origin from *salvo*, heal.

Dark Mullein *Verbascum nigrum*
Family: Scrophulariaceae

Habitat Dry grassy places, roadsides, usually calcareous.
Distribution Throughout most of Europe, including England (mainly east) and Wales.
Flowering-time June to September.
Description Mulleins are handsome plants with stately spikes of attractive flowers, erect and tall above a wealth of soft downy leaves. Usually biennial, they include some of the tallest herbaceous plants of Europe. Whether growing singly, in scattered clusters or forming a wonderfully crowded cummerbund as in our photograph, they beautify waste ground with a delightful combination of dignity and gaiety through summer into late autumn.

From a ground-hugging rosette of hairy leaves up to 30 cm (12 in) long grows the usually unbranched stem of *Verbascum nigrum*, 50 to 120 cm (20 in to 4 ft) tall. The upper part is densely packed with clear yellow flowers in clusters of 5 to 10, and from 12 to 22 mm ($\frac{1}{2}$ to 1 in) in diameter. These flowers are unusually fascinating. Their 5 rounded petals are united in the lower part with purple markings inside; 5 stamens alternate with them, their long filaments thickly clothed with beautiful purple hairs and topped with bright orange anthers.

Points of Interest Mulleins are hairy plants, this one less than most; their names stem from Latin *barbascum* 'bearded' and *mollis* 'soft'. They are reputed to possess anti-magical properties.

Meadow Saffron *Colchicum autumnale*
Family: Liliaceae

Habitat Damp meadows, calcareous and neutral soil.
Distribution Most of Europe except extreme north; England, Wales, Ireland (very rare).
Flowering-time August to October.
Description Just as we might be forgiven for thinking the season of wild flowers is over for the year, the late-cut meadows are transformed in autumn into scenes of wondrous delight with the silvery-purple sheen of colchicums, plants with a peculiar life cycle, and the equally peculiar name 'Naked Ladies'.

The 6 mauve petals are united into a long whitish tube (there is no visible stem) which conceals the ovary at its base. Here the seeds develop after fertilisation but not until spring do they ripen. The green capsule, 4 cm ($1\frac{1}{2}$ in), containing them can be seen in May and June just above ground-level within the circle of leaves, 20 to 25 cm (8 to 10 in) long. The seeds are dispersed and the leaves withered before the flower buds' autumnal appearance: as they are often produced in abundance this unusual timing appears to be highly successful.

Points of Interest Though similar in appearance to the genus *Crocus* and often misnamed 'Autumn Crocus' there are important differences. The colchicums have 6 stamens and 3 separate styles and stigmas, whereas the true crocuses possess only 3 stamens and a single 3-lobed style, the lobes bright orange and curly. These stigmas of *Crocus sativus* yield the yellow dye saffron, *not* the colchicum. *Colchicum* is notoriously poisonous to animals and humans.

Chicory *Cichorium intybus*
Family: Compositae

Habitat Roadsides, waste land, arable fields on chalk and limestone.
Distribution Widespread in the British Isles, but local in southern England and Wales, thinning out northward into Scotland, rare in Ireland. Found throughout most of Europe except the arctic regions.
Flowering-time July to October.
Description Chicory is a rather coarse, straggling plant but so beautifully bedecked with large wheel-like flower-heads whose 'spokes' are of the purest blue that they cannot readily be ignored or passed by. A few other members of Compositae delight the beholder with blue flowers (such as Alpine Sow-thistle and Blue Lettuce) but none possess the clear purity of colour and the size of those Chicory. Each flower-head opens independently in no particular order, and survives scarcely a day but for about three months there follows a continuous supply, each a gem of beauty in itself.

Usually, the plants are found in fair numbers lining a chalky roadside or colouring a spare corner of cultivated land where the dappled effect of the blue 'wheels' displays a fascinating pattern.

They are perennial, growing sturdily 60 to 90 cm (2 to 3 ft) tall from a long fleshy taproot and the grooved stalks are stiff, branched and spreading. Basal leaves form a ground-rosette and are short-stalked, rough and deeply lobed; stem leaves are smaller and narrower with pointed bases clasping the stem. The azure inflorescences $2\frac{1}{2}$ to 4 cm (1 to $1\frac{1}{2}$ in) across, and almost perfect in their circular outline, grow chiefly in the axils of the upper leaves, 2 or 3 together but rarely more than one of each group in bloom at once. They are almost stemless and lie closely flattened to the main stalk thus giving the overall blue-dappled effect already described.

Every flower head or inflorescence is composed of about 16 to 20 perfect florets, each one like a short blue strap with a squared 5-pointed outer end. These tiny points represent the 5 petals from which the strap is made. From the narrowed tubular base of the strap grow 5 stamens, their blue anthers united into a tube through which the style pushes before dividing into 2 stigmas, also blue. This arrangement is characteristic of *Compositae* and reveals another clever device to ensure cross-pollination by insects.
Points of Interest The large taproots of this species yield the chicory of commerce, a product which is mixed with coffee. The plants are widely cultivated for that purpose for which the roots are roasted and ground. When blanched, the crisp leaves of both this plant and its eastern relative *Cichorium endivia* are used as a salad vegetable. The name Chicory is of Arabic origin.

Fritillary *Fritillaria meleagris*
Family: Liliaceae

Habitat Water meadows and damp pastures.

Distribution Found in a few southern English counties, mainly in the upper Thames valley. Decreasing in Britain but found locally through most of Europe, from France to the Caucasus and northward to Scandinavia.

Flowering-time April to May.

Description There is something unique about a fritillary meadow; something that makes any effort to see one in full bloom so very worthwhile. Thousands of nodding maroon-pink flowers, not in a dense mass, but outlined separately at the height of the surrounding grass, make one of the most peculiarly enchanting floral-displays imaginable. Swaying gently in the soft spring breeze, or glowing warmly in the rays of the setting sun, nothing can quite equal the thrill of one's first sight of them. Few other plants flower with them; almost the only distraction from the soft dark bells is an occasional pure white form of the fritillaries themselves, which serves to enhance the exquisite loveliness of the multitude of coloured ones.

They are traditionally associated with water meadows where controlled winter flooding provided early spring grass for sheep and lambs, after which the fields were left ungrazed for summer hay. This management suited the fritillaries but now changing farming methods have altered the scene, and the plants are disappearing as a result of more intensive summer grazing, or of ploughing.

The plants are bulbous like many *Liliaceae*, slender-stalked from 25 to 45 cm (10 to 18 in) tall and with 4 or 5 narrow grasslike grey-green leaves. Usually there is one drooping flower with no green sepals but 6 petal-like parts from 3 to 4 cm (up to $1\frac{1}{2}$ in) long, slightly overlapping and pointed. Though basically bell-shaped the flowers are flat-topped and each petal has a raised central ridge giving the whole an angular rather than a rounded appearance. They are of a beautifully chequered design in two shades of maroon and pink, and they protect 6 yellow-anthered stamens and a single style with its 3 spreading stigmas.

Points of Interest The fascination of fritillaries has always tempted people to gather them, but now that so many water meadows have disappeared because of farming changes only special protection can keep those plants that are left. Fortunately, this protection is now officially given in some countries, but the co-operation of everyone by leaving the plants untouched is of tremendous value for their conservation for future generations.

The fritillary's chequered design is the origin of several names including the German *Schachblume* and French *Damier*. Fritillaria is from the Latin *fritillus*, a dice-box; *meleagris* is the Greek guinea-fowl whose feathers show a similar pattern, and Gerard in his *Herball* (1597) quaintly calls it 'Ginny-hen floure'. The sinister English Snake's-head refers to the appearance of the flower as it opens (see photograph). Finally the Dutch *Kievitsbloem* or 'Flower of the Lapwing' which likens the pattern to the marking of the eggs of that beautiful bird, gives a much more pleasing comparison.

Drooping Star-of-Bethlehem *Ornithogalum nutans*
Family: Liliaceae

Habitat Grassy and cultivated places, vineyards, olive groves.

Distribution In the British Isles, introduced and naturalised in a few places in the southern half of England. In Europe, native in the Mediterranean area, introduced elsewhere.

Flowering-time April, May.

Description The European Ornithogalums are most frequently found bespangling dry grassy or stony places with clusters of wide-open starry white flowers especially in Mediterranean lands. This particular species is handsome, tall and erect with a long inflorescence of large pendent flowers, greenish-white in colour, the petals being finely-pointed and of a delicate texture. Their grassy green haunts provide a perfect background for these slender spikes of pale beauty.

The stems reach a height of some 50 cm (20 in) and both they and the long grooved leaves grow from a 5 cm (2 in) bulb, and all are smooth and shining. The flowering-spikes are one-sided and carry up to 12 blooms, the lower ones being the first to open. Behind each flower is a papery-thin whitish-green bract, which is longer than the curving flower-stalk. The pointed buds are bluish-green and unfold into 6 separate petal-like parts spreading to form a star, white within but marked with a silvery-green band without. Six stamens, the number characteristic of *Liliaceae*, are here unusual in that the white stalks are each broad and flattened and the anther is located between 2 small points at the top. They form a circlet round the short style and the little group thus formed is easily distinguishable in the photograph.

Points of Interest *Ornithogalum* is a combination of two Greek words meaning 'Birds' Milk' supposedly referring to the way in which the more brilliant flowers of the related species *O. umbellatum* whiten rocky places around the Mediterranean like bird-droppings. This may be an imaginative comparison, but hardly complimentary to such a beautiful group of plants! Compensation is gained, however, by the use of Star-of-Bethlehem for the same plant which is very common in the Holy Land, and this name has been transferred to other members of the genus, including *O. nutans*.

Spring Snowflake *Leucojum vernum*
Family: Amaryllidaceae

Habitat Light woodland, damp places near streams, meadows in hills to 1600 m (5300 ft) as the snow melts. Occasionally naturalised as a relic of cultivation.

Distribution British Isles. Very rare, in southern England only in Britain, but fairly widespread and local in most of Europe.

Flowering-time February to April.

Description Together with the better-known and more common snowdrops, these charming little plants link the passing of winter with the onset of spring. Whether surrounded by cold melting snow in Europe's mountain pastures or snuggling in thick shining clumps beneath the leafless trees of an English woodland, their bright cheering presence marks the beginning of the year's display of exquisite beauty. Pure white flowers and fresh green leaves, one the colour of winter, the other of spring, provide their bleak background with a contrast as sharp and cold as the frosty wind itself.

They grow from bulbs as do many spring-flowering plants and make good use of this winter store of food by thrusting up several strong glossy leaves from 10 to 15 cm (4 to 6 in) long and about 10 mm ($\frac{1}{3}$ in) wide. Then the flowering stem emerges to grow taller than the leaves, up to 20 cm (8 in), and bearing one (rarely two) large drooping bell-shaped flower, $2\frac{1}{2}$ cm (1 in) long, with 6 petals equal in size and shape, broad and white except for the attraction of a yellow-green patch behind each pointed white tip. Inside the bell are 6 stamens of equal length displaying long golden anthers on shorter white filaments and encircling a thick white pistil tipped with green. Behind the flower is an oval smooth green ovary which later becomes the seed-capsule.

Points of Interest 'Snowflakes' (*Leucojum* species) and 'Snowdrops' (*Galanthus* species) belong to the same botanical family and appear much alike at first glance. They are the first conspicuous wild flowers to welcome the spring, grow in similar places and are all characterised by their white and green coloration. But there are differences; the leaves of the *Leucojums* are vivid glossy green and fairly broad while those of *Galanthus nivalis* (the common Snowdrop) are thin and bluish-green. The flowers of both are pendent, but whereas those of the snowflakes are bell-shaped with equal petals rather like pixies' hoods with their sharp points, the snowdrop flower has 3 outer comparatively narrow petals spreading beyond an inner circlet of 3 shorter ones.

Leucojum aestivum, Europe's other native snowflake, can also be distinguished from *L. vernum* in several ways. Its flowering time is later, April to May (hence its name of Summer Snowflake) and it likes wetter situations, on the edge of open water. The plants are taller, from 30 to 45 cm (1 to $1\frac{1}{2}$ ft) and each flowering-stem carries 3 to 6 flowers, drooping as in *L. vernum* and similar in shape and colouring but smaller, $1\frac{1}{2}$ to 2 cm ($\frac{1}{2}$ to $\frac{3}{4}$ in) on slender stalks of unequal length. The name *Leucojum* is of Greek origin meaning a white violet.

Foxglove *Digitalis purpurea*
Family: Scrophulariaceae

Habitat Woods, shady roadsides and clearings, heaths, on acid sandy soils.

Distribution Common throughout Britain, except on lime. Widespread in northern, central and south-western Europe.

Flowering-time June to August.

Description Foxgloves are to the summer landscape as primroses are to spring. Growing in similar shady situations they provide a glorious picture of abundant growth in one of the warmest flower-colours of the temperate world. Frequently they cover newly-disturbed ground provided by burning or the felling of trees where their dominant red spearheads may be present in thousands. Equally lovely are they when lining country lanes whose good hedges still provide that light shade which they enjoy. Normally, these colourful colonies are deep pinkish-red but a white variety occasionally introduces contrast and in parts of Scotland is co-dominant with the red or even supersedes it.

They dislike lime and on acid and dry sandy areas therefore, their rich beauty is compensation for the smaller variety of species found there.

They are biennial and the first year leaves form a large ground-rosette from which grow the handsome flower-spikes the following year. These are from 50 to 150 cm ($1\frac{1}{2}$ to 5 ft) tall, downy, unbranched and leafy. The leaves are fairly broad, soft and wrinkled, the beautiful tracery of network veins being very well-marked, especially beneath.

The one-sided flower-spike may clothe half the length of the stem with from 20 to 80 short-stalked flowers, each drooping from the axil of a leaflike bract. A closer look at one bell-like blossom (3 to 5 cm; 1 to 2 in) shows that it is slightly two-lipped, the lower somewhat larger and displaying a few finely-delicate hairs. The inner surface is boldly-patterned with dark red spots encircled with white rings which are honey-guides to ensure that bumble-bees reach the nectar at the base of the tube. Four stamens can be seen, 2 upper and 2 lower, and a slender style which later lengthens and is persistent on the seed-capsule, as the photograph shows. Foxgloves produce a tremendous number of small dry seeds; it has been estimated that one plant may have as many as 750,000.

Points of Interest This well-loved plant has collected a number of fanciful names connected with foxes, fairies – the mysterious 'little folk' – witches, and even with the Devil himself. *Digitalis* in Latin means a thimble and 'Devil's Thimble' is given by some people because of the plant's strongly poisonous character. By sharp contrast, it is one of the most valuable medicinal plants, when properly used by knowledgeable people. Drugs obtained from the leaves have been used in cases of heart complaints since the late eighteenth century, but long before then it was found to be of great benefit as an external application for wounds and ulcers.

The Foxglove is thus an excellent example of the many wild plants with a dual character and raises the interesting speculation as to how and when the human race discovered both their vices and their virtues.

Giant Bellflower *Campanula latifolia*
Family: Campanulaceae

Habitat Undisturbed woodlands, damp bushy places, banks of streams; on nutrient-rich soil.

Distribution In the British Isles from north-east Scotland to just south of the Thames, most plentiful in northern England; not in Ireland. In Europe, widely distributed south of 68° North to the Pyrenees and Alps; from the plains to sub-alpine regions.

Flowering-time July and August.

Description Amongst dense vegetation in sun-dappled woodlands, the graceful spikes of the Giant Bellflower rise tall and stately above tangled green undergrowth. Although occasionally solitary, the plants more frequently grow in small colonies, where their pale blue flowers appear almost ethereal in shady glens and glades. When they form part of the varied display along river or stream banks they provide a beautifully soft foil for the brighter colours of more common waterside species. By contrast, as sometimes happens with plants whose natural home is the rich soil of mature woodlands, they surprise us by making the best of a lush rootrun along an upland limestone wall as in our photograph.

Dignified and tall, up to 120 cm (4 ft) in height, these bell-flowers are perennial with furrowed downy unbranched stems well-clothed below with soft broad leaves and above with almost horizontal bell-like flowers. The basal leaves are stalked, about 15 cm (6 in) long, hairy and almost heart-shaped. Those on the stem are sessile, long, pointed and slightly toothed, gradually decreasing in size up the stem until they are replaced by leafy bracts which subtend the flowers. About 20 of these grow singly on short stalks, usually pale blue but occasionally white or darker blue forms appear. Although large, about 4 cm (1½ in) long and nearly as wide they exhibit a delicate porcelain appearance.

The 5 green sepals are long and pointed and the bell-like corolla ends in 5 reflexed points. Within the bell are 5 stamens which produce pollen before the 3 stigmas are ripe. Nectar is secreted at the base of the bell and only large long-tongued bees can reach this as fine hairs prevent smaller inquisitive but non-pollinating insects from crawling down.

Points of Interest The pollination mechanism of *Campanulaceae* and *Compositae*, two highly-developed plant families, is unusual and worth noting as applicable to *Campanula latifolia*. In a young flower, the 5 united stamens surround the style which lengthens, pushes up through the anthers and brushes pollen from them onto its own hairy surface. A nectar-seeking bee thus receives pollen from the style onto its body as it pushes down the bell. Later the 3 stigmas, so far closed, spread out to receive pollen brought from another plant, and cross-pollination is effectively accomplished. Should a flower be missed, the stigmas will curl back onto the style and collect any pollen remaining there so that seed may be set by means of self-pollination. In our photograph the lower flowers of the plant on the right show the stage at which the stigmas are outspread ready to receive pollen.

Herb Paris *Paris quadrifolia*
Family: Liliaceae

Habitat Damp woods, lowland to 2000 m (6600 ft).
Distribution Widespread but local throughout most of Europe, including the British Isles.
Flowering-time May to July.
Description Green amongst green – the peculiar flowers of Herb Paris tuck themselves away amongst the thick greenery of early summer in the woodlands, preferably calcareous. They can be recognised by the round black berry-like ovary in the centre of each single green star of a flower above a large four-pointed collar of leaves.

These sessile leaves spread horizontally and crosswise from the same point at the top of a glabrous slightly ridged stem, erect and from 15 to 30 cm (6 to 12 in) tall. The leaves are broadly oval, sharply pointed and about 8 cm (3 in) long, with net-veining strongly marked on both sides, quite unlike the typical parallel veins of most plants of *Liliaceae*.

From the same point on the stem as the leaves grows one small flower, shortly-stalked and unusual in form and colouring. Four green sepals about 3 cm (1¼ in) long alternate with 4 shorter very narrow yellow-green petals, all with a green stamen opposite. The central black berry at first is topped by black spreading stigmas and is about 6 mm (¼ in) in diameter, increasing to 14 mm (a good ½ in) when ripe.

Points of Interest *Quadrifolia* or 4-leaved is the rule but plants with 5 leaves occur. Nicholas Culpeper, the herbalist (1653) named this plant 'Herb True-Love'.

May Lily *Maianthemum bifolium*
Family: Liliaceae

Habitat Woods from plains to 2100 m (7000 ft).

Distribution Widespread most of Europe, local but sometimes abundant. Only England in the British Isles, and extremely rare.

Flowering-time May to July.

Description Woodlands are the home of a number of delightfully charming small plants, of which the May Lily is one of the daintiest. Tiny flowers cluster in close creamy foam, cool and soft in the dappled shade of green mossy hollows and boulders.

The perennial plants possess a creeping rhizome from which grow slender erect stems from 8 to 15 cm (3 to 6 in) tall and each with 2 heart-shaped leaves, the lower one nearly twice the size of the upper, 6 to 7 and $3\frac{1}{2}$ to 4 cm, respectively ($2\frac{1}{2}$ and $1\frac{1}{2}$ in). Above them a thin stem carries several small white flowers 5 m ($\frac{1}{4}$ in) wide each with 4 spreading petals, 4 stamens and an ovary which later enlarges to a seed-containing red berry.

Points of Interest The world distribution of the genus *Maianthemum* raises an interesting point for study. *M. bifolium* is widespread through Asia as well as Europe, but in the U.S.A. and Canada, it has a counterpart *Maianthemum canadense*, which though similar is sufficiently different for both to qualify for specific rank. This occurrence is not infrequent; the difference in geographical locations may be wide, as in this case, but not always.

Narrow-leaved Helleborine *Cephalanthera longifolia*
Family: Orchidaceae.

Habitat Calcareous woodland amongst beech, oak or ash trees up to 1370 m (4500 ft).

Distribution Scattered localities throughout but local and very rare in the British Isles. Widespread, locally in fair numbers in Europe.

Flowering-time May, June.

Description A colony of these vividly white orchids, stiffly erect, is a startling sight amongst the green undergrowth of light woodland, a thrilling discovery in one's plant-searching experiences. Their leafy stems are topped by a spike of flowers of such brilliance that the picture described is visible some distance away, small pools of whiteness in a green surround. Their upright stance and sharply-pointed narrow leaves produce a smart soldierly effect amongst vegetation which by contrast creeps, climbs and entwines itself into a complete tangle of tendrils, prickles, shrubs and grasses beneath the tall silent trees. It is here that these gems of the orchid-world grow sparingly in widely-scattered special localities.

Usually, each plant has a single stem, strong and smooth, from 15 cm (6 in) to 40 cm (16 in) tall and on which grow about 8 or 10 long sword-like leaves often in 2 rows and with slightly sheathing bases. The lower leaves are the shortest and widest, those in the middle the narrowest and longest – up to 14 cm ($5\frac{1}{2}$ in) and the top ones still narrow but becoming shorter again. The leaves give the plant its specific name *longifolia* which is repeated in the local name of most languages. The flower-spike lengthens above the leaves and is therefore conspicuous as already described, especially as the bracts characteristic of orchid inflorescences are here exceptionally small, thus allowing the white flowers even more prominence.

Each flower has 6 perianth-parts of equal length, the outer ones pointed, the inner more rounded. They are rarely fully wide open, although much more so than those of a related species *Cephalanthera damasonium* found in similar situations. Both plants exhibit deep yellow markings on the heart-shaped hairy lip, more easily seen in *C. longifolia*. The flowers are almost stalkless; the green part below the perianth is a twisted ovary which becomes the seed-pod after the flowers have been pollinated by insects, possibly small bees.

Points of Interest Most wild plants are found in greater abundance on the European mainland than in the British Isles. It is therefore interesting to note that whereas this applies to *Cephalanthera longifolia* the opposite seems to be the case with *C. damasonium*, which is borne out by our own experience. *C. damasonium* is widespread in southern England but a threatened species on a world-wide scale. *C. longifolia* is protected throughout Switzerland.

Limodore *Limodorum abortivum*
Family: Orchidaceae.

Habitat Woods, especially pine, bushy hillsides, shady banks on calcareous soil, from sea-level to 1200 m (4000 ft).

Distribution Local, rather rare in central and southern Europe, circum-Mediterranean. Not a British species.

Flowering-time May and June.

Description The Violet Birdsnest Orchid as this plant is sometimes named, has the advantage of easy identification. Its erect spikes of an unusual yet beautiful shade of lilac-purple free of all green colouring are quite unlike those of any other European orchid. Small colonies of almost ghostlike appearance grow in woodland clearings where the fresh green of grass and young bracken are a foil for their soft uniform shading. Above Mediterranean shores they are found amongst taller shrubby Lavender and Cistus where their gentle violet reflects the deeper purple and pink of these rich-flowering neighbours.

From deeply-buried underground stems these orchids grow to a height of 15 to 60 cm or more (6 in to 2 ft), often in small compact groups as in our photograph. The aerial stems are clothed with greyish-purple sheathing scales instead of green leaves, the lower ones almost overlapping. The buds, from 4 to about 20 in number, are erect and closely pressed to the stem, each in the axil of a bract similar to but shorter than the scales below. As the buds open the flowers turn to face outwards displaying magnificent colour and form which unfortunately is not long-lasting. The top petal is fairly broad and curving above the column which in orchids represents the stamens and stigma. Four narrow petals spread, winglike, sideways and the lower one forms a shallow lip with attractive upcurled wavy edges. Below this is a downward-pointing narrow spur about as long as the twisted ovary. All these are of a rich lilac colour finely veined with a darker shade. An unexpected bright contrast is provided by yellow shading on the lip. To be seen at their best these flowers need a wet spring; if that period is too dry the buds tend to wither before opening. But at their best they are truly exotic plants in miniature.

Points of Interest Limodorums pursue a peculiar way of life reflected in their lack of green. Most plants make their own food with the aid of sunlight and chlorophyll, the green colouring of leaves and stems. A few species have evolved a method of obtaining food already manufactured by their neighbours. There are two ways of doing this, one by tapping the supply of living plants and the other of decayed vegetation. Those plants which adopt the first course are parasites (see *Orobanche elatior* on page 95), the second are saprophytes (see *Corallorhiza trifida* on page 65). Usually it is clear to which group a plant belongs but authorities seem reluctant to decide in the case of *Limodorum*.

Twinflower *Linnaea borealis*
Family: Caprifoliaceae

Habitat Woods, especially pine, in mountains and tundra.
Distribution Northern Europe including Scotland; local in mountains.
Flowering-time July, August.
Description Carl Linnaeus must have seen thousands of delicate pink blossoms on his pioneering Lapland journey, as they hung demurely above their carpet of trailing leafy stems amongst ground mosses and lichens.

These woody stems produce several leafy branches from which grow thin aerial flowering stems 5 to 10 cm (2 to 4 in) tall. Two bell-like flowers, 1 cm (scarcely $\frac{1}{2}$ in) long hang from the top of each stem (hence Twinflower); they are delicate pink with darker lines and delightfully fragrant. Numerous attractive small leaves grow in pairs and are almost round, slightly indented and darker above than beneath.

Points of Interest We are indebted to Carl Linnaeus (1707–1778) for the comparatively simple binomial method of naming plants and animals which replaced the complicated descriptions previously adopted. He delighted in honouring the work of his contemporaries by incorporating their names in those of the plants (see *Bartsia alpina* on page 131), and it is good therefore that his own name should be perpetuated likewise. On the instigation of a distinguished Dutch botanist *J. Grovonius* he chose and named this lowly but beautiful little plant of the north for himself.

Alpine Clematis *Clematis alpina*
Family: Ranunculaceae

Habitat Subalpine woodlands, rocky places, from 900 to 2300 m (3000 to 7500 ft).
Distribution Central European Alps. Not British.
Flowering-time June, July.
Description Travellers Joy is such a happy name for the festooned feathery seedheads of *Clematis vitalba* the widespread lowland relative of this exquisite alpine climber. *C. alpina* is also a joy to summertime wanderers who find its falling cascades of violet-purple flowers amongst the dark needle-leaves and brown cones of the mountain pines. Later thousands of seedplumes catch the autumn sunlight producing curtains of shimmering silver.

Though woody at the base the plants' perennial stems are weak and from 1 to $3\frac{1}{2}$ m ($3\frac{1}{4}$ to 10 ft) long. The leaves are unevenly divided into toothed lobes on slender stalks 3 to 4 cm (between 1 and 2 in) long. The solitary flowers each have 4 large purple sepals, folded in bud, outspread later. Within them is a circle of white strap-shaped nectaries to attract insects, a ring of gold-topped stamens and a central cluster of pistils.
Points of Interest This is the only climbing plant of the Alps; each spring it pulls up its weak stems, fresh leaves and ethereally lovely flowers over stronger plants, often pinetrees, by means of last year's leafstalks. After leaf-fall these stalks become hard and wiry and so sensitive to touch that contact with a possible supporting stem or twig immediately stimulates them to curl around it and hold fast.

Alpine Columbine *Aquilegia alpina*
Family: Ranunculaceae

Habitat Subalpine, on steep stony slopes of grassland and light woodland from 1200 to 2600 m (4000 to 9000 ft).

Distribution From the western Alps of France through Switzerland to the Vorarlberg in Austria. Northern Apennines. Uncommon and local.

Flowering-time July and August.

Description A rare plant of great beauty whose large pendent flowers of a wonderful clear blue present a picture of ethereal loveliness when seen amongst the greenery of a steep sunlit hillside. On open slopes devoid of trees, the plants are found near boulders around which there is a cool rootrun and which provide some shade. The background for the blue and white flowers is then the blue and white sky, as they sway in the ever-blowing mountain breeze.

These aquilegias are numbered amongst the tall mountain perennials reaching a height of 25 to 40 cm (10 to 18 in), in competition with other more common woodland species. The stems carry from one to three flowers 5 to 8 cm (2 to 3 in) across, each with five large spreading blue sepals. The petals, also five in number, are about half the size of the sepals and form an inner circlet ranging from deep blue to creamy-white in colour. Each one ends in a blunt curved backward-pointing spur about 18 mm ($\frac{3}{4}$ in) long. The spurs contain nectar, the food of bees whose tongues are long enough to reach the base.

The petals surround a bunch of numerous stamens and five central pistils which mature at different times so that the nectar-seeking bees can effect cross-pollination.

The beauty of the plant is enhanced by its many slender-stalked leaves which are large and three-lobed, each lobe being deeply indented to give a delicate fernlike appearance.

Points of Interest It is not surprising that this, one of the most rare and beautiful mountain plants, has been the victim of much over-collecting in the past. It has nevertheless long been a protected plant in its Alpine stations and should be left completely undisturbed. Then the plants can multiply by the continuous production of seed – lost if the flowers are picked – and, by remaining, give continued joy to other people. The spectacular reproduction of a blue flower against a background of blue sky, as seen in our picture, and described in the text, is a point worth noting, as blue does not always correctly register on colour film, but in this case has been achieved to perfection.

Willow Gentian *Gentiana asclepiadea*
Family: Gentianaceae

Habitat Subalpine. Bushy places, light woodland, to 2200 m (6800 ft) on calcareous soil.
Distribution Endemic to the hills and mountains of central and southern Europe, local.
Flowering-time July to October.
Description

> 'The dawn descending kissed awake blue stars
> Of Gentians – –'

F. W. Bourdillon.

Hardly a scientific approach to the evolution of plants perhaps, but who will argue that point at the first magical moment of seeing these flowers of so wonderful and exquisite a blue? Innumerable species of gentians (though not all blue) transform the world's mountains into a vast casket of jewels, and to use the word enraptured to describe one's feelings at first sight of them is no exaggeration. Although it may be, as it frequently is, a vivid carpet of spring gentians in an alpine meadow which gives us our earliest greeting, it is equally thrilling to find the rarer types, including the Willow gentians of the mountain woodlands. And as they bloom later in the season they imbue the autumnal tinge of the woods with a rich remnant of summer, prolonging its stay with their deep blue flowers.

Gentiana asclepiadea is a perennial with a leafy stem from 20 to 50 cm (8 to 20 in) tall, usually erect, but sometimes curving into a graceful arch, especially in the more shady parts of its habitat. All leaves grow on the stem in pairs; they are stalkless, rather narrow, and with well-defined veining. The intensely blue flowers are borne in the axils of the upper leaves in clusters of 1 to 3 together and up to about 30 in number. Each has a small green 5-partite calyx surrounding the base of the long narrow tubular corolla which ends in 5 spreading starlike points. Within the tube (3 to 5 cm or $1\frac{1}{4}$ to 2 in long), the blue is variably patterned with pale stripes and purplish spots, whilst very rarely pure white flowers occur.

Points of Interest A one-time King of Illyria in eastern Europe, who died in the year 167 B.C., was the first person to realise the medicinal value of gentian roots (of the related species *G. lutea*) and use them in the treatment of plague. The King's name was Gentius and for him this whole genus of plants, all so beautiful, and some so useful, is named. Our plant's specific name *asclepiadea* refers to its leaves which resemble those of a genus of herbaceous plants *Asclepias* (family *Asclepiadaceae*) found chiefly in North America. They are also similar to the leaves of Willow trees, hence the English name Willow Gentian. It is a protected plant in Switzerland.

Lady's-slipper *Cypripedium calceolus*
Family: Orchidaceae

Habitat Subalpine. Light woodland, chiefly coniferous in Europe, often on steep slopes; on calcareous soil. To 2000 m (7000 ft).

Distribution In Britain, northern England only and almost extinct. Widespread in hilly districts but very local in Europe.

Flowering-time Between May and July.

Description This, the largest European orchid, is a plant of exotic beauty and fascination giving the impression of having strayed from some faraway tropical forest into Europe's cool subalpine woods so refreshingly dappled with sun and shade. Many lovely plants share its terrain, globeflowers, lily of the valley, Herb Paris and a variety of smaller orchids, but in elegance the proud and stately Lady's-slipper reigns over all.

Usually each plant has one large strikingly lovely flower (occasionally there may be 2) on a long slender stem 15 to 50 cm (6 to 20 in) tall with 3 or 4 broad slightly sheathing leaves. The uppermost leaf stands erect behind the flower and all are bright green with strongly-marked parallel veins. The focal point of each flower is the shining yellow inflated lip which resembles a sabot type of shoe and is surrounded by 4 long maroon petals, pointed and often twisted. The widest petal is upright behind the lip, 2 narrow ones spread sideways and the fourth hangs behind and below the lip. This one consists of 2 fused petals, the evidence being visible in 2 tiny points at its tip, thus the flower reveals the total complement of 6 perianth-parts usual in orchids.

The golden slipper has a comparatively small opening on its upper surface, spotted with maroon, and where the column is visible. In wet weather the petals bend over the lip, especially the broad upper one and thus protect the precious organs of reproduction. This fact is clearly demonstrated in our photograph taken after a shower of snow.

Cross-pollination is effected by small bees which crawl into the slipper in search of nectar.

Points of Interest There is no doubt that the numbers of Lady's-slippers have diminished greatly wherever they grow within reach of people, who have uprooted them for private pleasure, and for commercial sale. They are now strictly protected by law in most European countries including Great Britain, but if 'almost extinct' is not to be written against all of Europe, as it already is written against England, then every person fortunate enough to find these wonderful plants, must be content to admire, and leave them as complete and as beautiful as they found them.

Cypripedium is taken from the Greek name for the goddess Venus. According to legend she took shelter from a storm and while running into the woods lost her gold and purple slipper. Later a mountain shepherdess found it but as she stooped to pick it up, it vanished. There instead was this flower of exquisite beauty.

Coralroot *Corallorhiza trifida*
Family: Orchidaceae

Habitat Damp mossy woodlands especially in the mountains; also tundra and sand-dune slacks.

Distribution Uncommon in Scotland and Northern England, but local in northern, central and western Europe.

Flowering-time May to August, according to situation.

Description These unusual little plants may easily pass unnoticed because of their small size and pale colouring. Beneath the dark pines of the forest and through its mossy carpet they appear in small colonies more akin to tiny ghosts than healthy living plants. But a moment's closer look at them will reveal in miniature the beauty of the delicately marked flowers drooping on thin leafless stems.

There are no roots; instead an underground stem develops twisted knobbly branches resembling coral, from which we have the generic name *Corallorhiza* in addition to several national names of the same meaning. A single slender yellow-green stem grows above ground about 10 to 25 cm (4 to 10 in) tall, leafless, but with a few small yellowish sheathing scales. The loose inflorescence comprises from 4 to 10 straw-yellow flowers on short stalks and subtended by tiny colourless bracts.

Each flower, though so small, is typically orchid-like in form with 6 perianth segments, the lowest and largest a hanging lip, the uppermost erect and rather broad and the remaining 4 are narrow and curving downwards. The only real colour of the plant is provided by a few red-brown marks on the flowers especially on the lip.

Points of Interest *C. trifida* is a saprophytic plant which obtains its nutriment directly from dead and decaying plant material, in this case the humus formed from fallen tree-leaves which surround it. There are no roots to absorb water and nutrient elements from the soil as in normal plants. Terrestrial orchids – those growing directly from the earth as are all European species – live in partnership with a fungus below ground. This takes the form of a tangle of thin threadlike rambling branches which penetrate those of the orchid rootstock. They are able to absorb liquid food directly from the plant remains and pass it on to the rhizome of *Corallorhiza*. When sufficient food is stored in the rootstock – and not until – the flowering stem appears above ground. Because of this arrangement, these orchids have no need of chlorophyll, the source of green colour in plants and which is an essential factor in their normal synthesising of food. Therefore saprophytes are usually less colourful in appearance than their neighbours of more conventional habits.

Water Crowfoot *Ranunculus peltatus*
Family: Ranunculaceae

Habitat Aquatic. Ponds, lake margins, slow-flowing streams.
Distribution Widespread through Europe and British Isles.
Flowering-time May to July.
Description How lovely in May to see the shining flowers of water-crowfoot bespangling ponds and streams of the countryside with a multitude of islands, white and emerald green. Masses of clear white blossoms, whose erect slender stalks thrust them upwards above water-level, wave gently with the wind on the lazy current to produce an enchanting picture which captures perfectly the delicate freshness of early summer.

Ranunculus peltatus is one of several species of water crowfoot, difficult to sort out separately, but readily recognised as a group. They are all aquatic with stems up to 6 m (19$\frac{1}{2}$ ft) long lying horizontally beneath the water. Some possess surface floating leaves, glossy and flat with a waxy surface to throw off surplus water. Others have an underwater network of finely-cut delicate fronds which are beautifully adapted to move with the current and breathe from the water's oxygen supply. Some species have both types and a few can produce whichever kind best suits their surroundings. The flowers vary in size between species from $\frac{1}{2}$ to 3 cm (to 1$\frac{1}{4}$ in) but all possess 5 small green sepals, 5 white petals with a golden base and a centrepiece of numerous stamens and pistils.

Ranunculus peltatus normally exhibits both types of leaves and the photograph shows a typical view of it with large flowers and floating leaves in evidence.

Water Lobelia *Lobelia dortmanna*
Family: Lobeliaceae

Habitat and Distribution Aquatic. In gravelly lakes and tarns with acid water, chiefly in mountains. Locally common in suitable places throughout the British Isles and in western Europe from Brittany to southern Scandinavia.

Flowering-time June to August.

Description Picture a lonely mountain tarn, its dark waters ruffled by a lively breeze which sends cloud-shadows sailing across the slopes of the rock-strewn fells. The surface of the tarn is broken by many slender spikes of the peculiar water lobelia. Not spectacular plants these, with only a few singly-placed pale purple flowers on each unbranched stem, but how well their pale simplicity suits their wild setting.

Their perennial roots are firm in the gravelly mud of the shallow margins of these mountain lakes. From them arise tufts of smooth bright green leaves which usually remain completely submerged, each from 2 to 5 cm ($\frac{3}{4}$ to 2 in) long, linear and slightly recurved. Only the flowering-stems appear above water in summer with from 2 to 8 drooping pale lilac flowers. These flowers are tubular, slit along the top and irregularly divided at the lip into 5 parts, and are pollinated by long-tongued bees.

Points of Interest The leaves are peculiar in that each one is formed of 2 hollow tubes joined together. This wonderful engineering feat of nature enables them to withstand the strong currents and wind-blown waves which frequently arise in these desolate mountain waters.

Flowering-rush *Butomus umbellatus*
Family: Butomaceae

Habitat Aquatic; margins of lakes, ponds and slow-flowing rivers and canals.

Distribution In Britain widespread in the lowlands, mostly England but not common. Occurs throughout lowland Europe, local, not common. Possibly becoming more scarce everywhere.

Flowering-time July to September.

Description Although the stems and leaves of this plant may be rushlike in appearance, there the resemblance ends and it is not even a member of the rush family. It is adapted to an aquatic life and is found only around and in the shallows of lakes and slow-flowing water. It is therefore a plant of the plains and lowlands and its umbels of exquisite pink flowers swaying gently above surrounding summer greenery form one of the most exciting and beautiful rewards for the waterside wanderer. Unfortunately the plants, never very common, are becoming more scarce as their habitat disappears under the hand of man, and a really large colourful group is now a comparatively rare sight. But even one spreading flower-head is enchantingly lovely.

The perennial plants are firmly anchored in the wet oozy mud of the waterside by fleshy rhizomes, and the spreading clusters of softly-shaded flowers are held aloft on stout leafless stems up to 1.5 m (5 ft) tall. In each cluster about 20 separate flowers grow on slender stalks of varying lengths and together they exhibit all stages of development from buds to ripening carpels and all shades of pink from pale rose to deep maroon.

Each flower is $2\frac{1}{2}$ cm (1 in) across with 6 perianth-parts veined darker and 9 stamens whose red anthers turn black after shedding their orange pollen. In the centre are 6 carpels united at the base where nectar is secreted. Flying insects which come for the nectar carry away the pollen also, which is deposited upon the riper stigmas of another flower. Later the seeds are dispersed by water.

Points of Interest The sharp-edged leaves which can injure the mouths of cattle are responsible for the name *Butomus* which is from a Greek word meaning 'to cut'.

The rhizomes are edible and have been eaten in times of food shortage in the past, as is the case with several other wild plants.

Branched Bur-reed *Sparganium erectum*
Family: Sparganiaceae

Habitat Aquatic; in muddy edges and shallow water of slow-flowing rivers, canals and lakesides, from the plains to the foothills.

Distribution All Europe including the British Isles. Common throughout most areas in suitable habitats.

Flowering-time June to August.

Description So many tall colourful plants line the water's edge in summertime that the Bur-reed attracts attention simply by contrast, just because of its lack of bright colour and the peculiarity of its flowers which hardly resemble flowers at all. But they are worth a second look, first to enjoy the contrasting pattern of yellow-green spiky balls partly concealed by long overtopping leaves, then to see more closely – with a hand-lens if possible – exactly what is the composition of these odd-looking members of the flower-world.

Rooted deep in mud these perennial plants are strong with thick round erect stems arising to about 60 cm (2 ft) above the surface of mud or water before giving rise to a few short side-branches, scarcely spreading, on which grow the flower-heads. The leaves which sheathe the lower stem are much longer, reaching from 1 to 1.5 m (40 to 60 in) and being almost erect they surround the flower-heads lower down. Occasionally, some leaves may float on the water's surface. The flowering-stems grow in the axils of leaf-like bracts, the lowest being the longest. All leaves and stems are bright green, smooth and shining, the long leaves 2 cm ($\frac{3}{4}$ in) wide, flat on the upper surface and strongly keeled below.

To return to the flower-heads with a lens we find that each is tightly-packed with many small sessile flowers. The upper smaller and more numerous heads consist of male flowers possessing stamens, usually 3, and the lower are female, each flower having one green ovary. The hidden petals, 3 or 6, are like tiny scales. When all the stamens are yellow with pollen, or the large lower balls are each covered with about 50 protruding white styles and stigmas the whole spike is extremely attractive.

The male flowers quickly drop away after pollination, but the female balls then develop into the hard green spiky fruits which give the name 'bur' – reed to the plants. The flowers are wind pollinated and the seeds dispersed on the water where they can float for some time.

Marsh Helleborine *Epipactis palustris*
Family: Orchidaceae

Habitat Marshy ground, fens, dune-slacks, where the water is alkaline.

Distribution British Isles. Widespread and locally common in England, Wales and Ireland; sparingly in southern Scotland.

Europe. Through most of Europe; not the extreme north, and rare in the Mediterranean. Most frequent in lowland areas, but does reach 1525 m (5000 ft) in the Alps.

Flowering-time June to August.

Description One of the most attractive European orchids is the pale helleborine of the marshes, so different from all others of its genus in appearance and habitat, and therefore not difficult to identify. Individually, the flowers are exquisite and as their annual flowering is reasonably reliable, a journey to see them in the full summer display is always well-rewarded. Across the marsh some hundreds of frilled and delicately tinted nodding flowers form a delightful and refreshing picture amongst the monotony of reeds or sphagnum, or above the silver-grey creeping willow of the flat dune-slacks.

The plants of inland marshes vary in height from 15 to 50 cm (6 to 20 in) while those found in coastal dune-slacks are usually shorter, averaging 15 cm (6 in) and more compact as the surrounding vegetation is also less tall than its inland counterpart. They grow from creeping underground stems and frequently appear, several flowering-stems together, in close groups, which is part of their charm. The leaves, 4 to 8 in number, are broad, the lower ones spreading, the upper sheathing the purple-tinted stem and becoming gradually shorter towards the top.

The really distinctive parts are the flowers, from about 8 to 20 in a loose somewhat one-sided raceme on short purple-shaded stalks and subtended by bracts of a similar colour and slightly longer than them. The flowers open more widely than those of most *Epipactis* species and differ from them also in their display of mingled delicate colourings instead of the plainer green, pink or red of their relatives. Greyish-purple, yellow-brown and white shade into one another on the pointed spreading sepals and petals and the characteristic orchid-lip has two distinct parts joined by a hinge. The cup-shaped upper half is yellow and white, and the larger lower half, white and frilled at the edges, spreads outward. In the flower's centre a touch of brightness is provided by the yellow pollinia.

Points of Interest All this is more than just beauty, good though that is. The attraction of the right type of insect, in this case hive bees, to effect cross-pollination is the fundamental need, and here our species differs again from all other *Epipactis* plants. The unusual flower structure leads to an ingenious and effective method by which the bee, on alighting on the lip is pushed by the action of the hinge into position to receive the pollen on its head. This is then transported to another flower where the stigma is in the right place to receive the pollen as the bee pushes its head inside.

Grass of Parnassus *Parnassia palustris*
Family: Parnassiaceae

Habitat Marshes, damp heaths, wet meadows, dune-slacks.

Distribution Locally common in Britain, throughout most of Scotland, north-west England, East Anglia, North Wales and most of mid-west Ireland; rare or absent elsewhere. Also locally common in suitable places through most of Europe, up to 2500 m (8000 ft).

Flowering-time Late July to October, depending upon situation.

Description Grämen Parnassi – Grass of Parnassus – how came this clear white flower of the mud and the marshland to acquire such a poetic yet seemingly ill-fitting name? It certainly is no grass; that fact is obvious on seeing its leaves; and what is its connection with the famous Greek mountain? But, whatever its origin, most Europeans are within reach of the delightful display of these exquisite flowers which transform and lighten the monotonous marshland scene as the late summer days decline with the approach of autumn.

The plants are lightly rooted in the wet soil but firmly anchored by a short underground stem from which spring from 1 to about 6 flowering stems and several heart-shaped leaves on stalks of varying lengths. Thus each leaf receives its share of light and is held clear of the surrounding mud. On each flowering-stem is one sessile leaf, also heart-shaped, a short way above ground-level. All the leaves are light green, smooth, shining, and about 2 cm ($\frac{3}{4}$ in) long. The flowers, 3.5 cm ($1\frac{1}{4}$ in) diameter, grow singly at the top of each slender stem and are almost flat except for the shallowly upturned edges of the petals. Five pale green sepals alternate with 5 broad white petals, notched at the rounded apex and enhanced by delicate green veins. Within the flower 5 normal stamens alternate with the petals and between them are 5 strange looking structures which are modified stamens. These are small white scales fringed with hairs, yellow-tipped and outspread; they are the nectar-secreting organs to which insects, mostly flies, are attracted. A central round green (or pinkish) ovary with 4 sessile stigmas on top, completes the picture.

Points of Interest The normal stamens produce pollen and ripen successively. In turn they become erect and shed their pollen away from the stigmas so that it becomes attached to the legs of visiting insects and removed to another flower whose stigmas are ripe. The stamens of the first flower bend outward again after losing their pollen and the stigmas ripen to receive pollen from a different flower. This is yet another fascinating method of ensuring cross-pollination.

As with *Pyrola rotundifolia* (page 9) and *Epipactis palustris* (page 73) there are two forms of this beautiful plant which sometimes shares the willow-carpeted sand-dune slacks with them. The coastal plants are shorter, less slender, and possess larger flowers than those of the inland marshes.

Marsh Gentian *Gentiana pneumonanthe*
Family: Gentianaceae

Habitat Wet heaths, bogs, marshes, avoiding lime.

Distribution Sparingly in northern-central and southern England, North Wales; diminishing. Local through much of Europe to 1200 m (4000 ft), mainly central.

Flowering-time July to October.

Description In singing the praises of the brilliant mountain gentians, as we rightly do, we should never forget the sheer loveliness of these gems of the autumn marshland. The blue of their skyward pointing flowers is so soft yet bright and deep that it would seem the blue September sky above them has deliberately let fall samples of itself onto these wild stretches of damp heathland. They stand slight and erect amongst marsh grasses and greyish foliage of pink Bell-heather (*Erica tetralix*) so that their presence is betrayed only by the uplifted beautiful funnels of blue. Like most gentians they are flowers of sunshine and warmth needing a temperature of 19°C (66°F) to display their full beauty. To see them at their glorious best it is therefore necessary to choose a mellow autumn day when the low sun's rays transform the flowers into translucent chalices of ethereal blue.

Though slender and rather delicate in appearance the plants are perennial with spreading roots which anchor them firmly in the boggy ground. The red-brown single stems, from 15 to 30 cm (6 to 12 in) are clothed with narrow paired leaves, darker green above than beneath, the lowest ones tiny, the upper ones reaching $2\frac{1}{2}$ cm (1 in) long.

Small plants are crowned with one erect flower but larger ones carry up to six flowers, shortly stalked in the axils of the upper leaves, and all clustered together near the top of the plant. A reddish calyx-tube divided into 5 pointed sepals surrounds the base of each funnel-shaped corolla which is composed of 5 petals united into a tube 3 to 3.5 cm (1 to $1\frac{1}{2}$ in) long and spreading starlike above in sunshine. At other times the petals appear spirally closed. The blue colouring (rarely very pale blue or white) is marked with muted green streaks and spots.

A look inside a young flower discloses 5 white anthers encircling the style and long narrow ovary. The stamens mature first and after losing their pollen to probing bumble-bees the white stigmas push through the anther-tube and spread out to receive pollen from another plant. The green markings and translucent effect of the flower tube are said to help in guiding the bees to the nectar at its inner base. Thus again are beauty and a practical need efficiently combined.

Points of Interest This is another beautiful plant which merits special protection; its numbers have already been much reduced because of extensive reclamation of its moorland habitat. Switzerland at least has it on its protected list and in Great Britain it is included in the law against uprooting of wild plants.

Pitcherplant *Sarracenia purpurea*
Family: Sarraceniaceae

Habitat Wet acid peat-bogs.
Distribution Native to North America, but introduced to Europe; abundantly naturalised in central Ireland; western Switzerland.
Flowering-time May to July.
Description Excitingly, though rarely, the sombre brownish-green of bogland may assume a peculiar lambent glow where hundreds of *Sarracenias* display their pitcher-like leaves in a marvellously mottled design of yellow, green and purple-red.

These collect water in which insects are drowned and their nutrient parts absorbed to supplement a deficient diet.

Above the leaves are from 1 to 4 erect stems, 20 to 40 cm (8 to 16 in) and bearing one large drooping flower, 5 cm (2 in) across, with 5 sepals and 5 petals, again coloured green and purple-red. In the centre is a large green stigma, resembling an open umbrella, which covers and protects numerous stamens and their pollen.

Points of Interest These extraordinary insectivorous plants of the New World have long fascinated European horticulturalists and the name *Sarracenia* honours Dr Michel Sarrasin de L'Etang, physician to the court of Quebec, who is reputed to have sent the first specimens to Europe. Their introduction to Ireland in the wild state was not until 1906.

Sarracenia purpurea is the national flower of Newfoundland.

Bog Asphodel *Narthecium ossifragum*
Family: Liliaceae

Habitat Acid bogs, wet heaths.
Distribution Widespread, often abundant in northern and western areas of Europe, including the British Isles.
Flowering-time July, August.
Description Over the heather-clad moors the continuous background of purple-green is dappled and broken by pools of peaty water. The spongy land around them is wet with moss and it is here we find the glorious golden spikes of Bog Asphodel like bright little lamps lighting the moorland way. Their lily-like flowers possess the most fascinating stamens whose filaments are softly clothed with yellow hairs, above which the curving anthers are thick with orange pollen.

The plant's woody rhizome threads through the mud and peat beneath the moss and produces a stiffly erect stem 10 to 30 cm (4 to 12 in) tall, and a basal tuft of somewhat shorter sword-like leaves. About 6 to 12 starry flowers are clustered in a fairly tight spike; each flower has 6 narrow petals, pale green outside, brilliant gold within and spreading starlike as they open. Spreading with them, one to each petal, are the stamens, slightly shorter, with yellow-furred filaments and fairly large anthers. The central ovary is bottle-shaped and pointed, elongating in fruit. After flowering the whole plant (stem, persistent petals and ovary) darkens to a beautiful tawny orange colour splashing the autumn bogland.

Common Cottongrass *Eriophorum angustifolium*
Family: Cyperaceae

Habitat Acid bogs and marshes, shallow pools, from the plains to 2700 m (9000 ft).

Distribution Widespread throughout Britain, especially north and west. Widespread in Europe except southern Mediterranean region. Locally abundant.

Flowering-time April to July, with seed-time June to September.

Description Very few people will ever notice the flowers of Cottongrass; it is not until the fluffy white balls of cotton – the seedheads – appear that the plants are conspicuous and then how miraculously do they transform their bogland home. These wide wet stretches of acid peat often appear monotonous because their flora is greatly restricted by poor soil conditions. A few colourful flowers are found sparingly such as Marsh Gentian and Bog Rosemary, but the chief colour and life of the bog are provided by a very limited number of species of which Cottongrass is one. At the height of its glory thousands upon thousands of delicately beautiful seedheads dance over the vast sombre carpet of sodden peat like snowflakes in the summer wind.

From a creeping rhizome the plants grow some 20 to 60 cm (8 in to 2 ft) tall, each with a single slender rounded stem and a few sheathing leaves which are very narrow, only about 4 mm across. They are deeply grooved, making them almost triangular in outline and are green in winter, though often dead by flowering-time.

The sedge-like flower-heads, from 3 to 7 in number, form a loose cluster on thin stalks of varying lengths, from 1 to 2 cm (up to $\frac{3}{4}$ in), and the whole inflorescence is subtended by a long pointed bract. Papery greyish-brown bracts surround the small individual spikelets, which are brightened at flowering-time by a display of protruding yellow anthers.

Later each tiny red-brown seed possesses its own tuft of silky hairs up to 3 cm (1.25 in) long and it is when these tufts are fully developed that the plants catch the eye with their multitudinous nodding balls of fluff. In due time these become detached and float away in the wind thus disseminating the seeds in all directions.

Points of Interest Despite its name this plant is not a true grass but belongs to the sedge family, *Cyperaceae* and thus differs in several ways from the grasses, including the similarly plumed Feather-grass, *Stipa pennata* (page 146). Though both these species have evolved a similar method of wind seed-dispersal, some important differences between the families are worth noting. Sedges nearly always live in wet places; grasses prefer dry ones, a fact well demonstrated by these two plants. The sheathing leaves of sedges form a complete tube around the stem whereas those of grasses are only folded around and split down one side. Grass stems are hollow, sedge stems usually solid or containing pith and they are nearly always triangular, Cottongrass being one of the few exceptions. Small but structurally important differences in the flowers require a lens and expert knowledge to unravel.

The seed-heads have been used, though not commercially, for stuffing pillows and making candle-wicks.

Dorset Heath *Erica ciliaris*
Family: Ericaceae

Habitat Bogs and heaths, open pine woods; avoids lime.

Distribution Local in south west England; very rare in western Ireland. Local in western areas of France, Spain and Portugal.

Flowering-time June to September.

Description Most members of the large genus *Erica* are attractive evergreen shrubs and the rare *Erica ciliaris* is no exception; indeed at the height of its flowering it is extremely beautiful, combining a rich array of large rose-pink flowers with fresh bright green foliage in a delightfully neat pattern of growth. The one-sided flowering spikes are quite distinctive, tapering gracefully like miniature spires especially when young, and as these are of varying heights the plants assume a pleasing design in outline. This arrangement ensures the maximum amount of light for leaves and flowers and possibly assists nectar-hunting bees.

The mingling of these richly-tinted flowers with those of more widespread species of heaths provides the typical moorland harmonious symphony of pink and purple, often stretching for miles, and perhaps broken occasionally by brilliant splashes of golden late flowering gorse (*Ulex minor* and *U. gallii*). A wonderful picture of glowing warmth before the imminence of winter.

From a woody base grows a tuft of brown stems from 15 to 45 cm (6 to 18 in) tall, leafy and much-branched. The leaves, in whorls of 3, are crowded on short side branches, more sparse on the main twigs and although hardly 3 mm long are quite fascinating when seen through a lens. They are bright green above, paler below, with recurved margins outlined with silvery glandular hairs like an array of minute clubs.

Above the leaves rise the rosy flowers (rarely white), urn-shaped and about 20 to a spike. In bud they droop, becoming more or less horizontal as they open. They average 1 cm long and have 4 small hairy sepals. The corolla tube narrows to a constricted 4-petalled opening from which protrudes a pink style and stigma, and just below them within the tube is a circle of 8 brown anthers. After pollination by bees the pink corolla turns tawny-brown, remaining for some time after the seeds ripen.

Points of Interest Heathlands or moorlands are based on expanses of acid peaty soil deficient in nitrogen, so necessary for normal growth. Plants living in these conditions must develop some unusual quality or mode of growth to combat this shortage. *Calluna vulgaris* (heather) and the *Erica* species have established a working partnership with certain fungi, which live in their roots, and can make the nitrogen in the air pockets of the soil available to their host-plant. From the host the fungus obtains other vital products in exchange and thus the partnership benefits both.

Bog Rosemary *Andromeda polifolia*
Family: Ericaceae

Habitat Peat-bogs.

Distribution Scattered in suitable localities in central and northern England, southern Scotland, central Ireland, rare in Wales. Central and northern Europe to the Arctic coast. Decreasing throughout much of its range, including Britain, due to land reclamation.

Flowering-time May and June.

Description Wide stretches of peat-bog tend to be dull and monotonous to the sight through most of the year and only when the white dancing heads of cottongrass or the purple carpeted heaths (*Erica*) appear in quantity is the landscape beautiful. However, in pockets of really wet ground some of Europe's most attractive and fascinating plants find the black peaty moss-filled home to their liking, or, more accurately, they have become adapted to it. Bog Rosemary is one of these, not always in great quantity in its southern range, but sometimes gloriously widespread especially in Arctic regions. That great Swedish botanist, Carl Linnaeus himself was captivated by the charm of its pale rosy waxen flowers which adorn the peat-bogs of Lapland with cluster upon cluster of delicate pink-suffused pearls.

From a creeping underground rootstock grow brown tough leafy stems, more or less erect, and carrying these lovely pink blossoms just above the highest evergreen leaves. These leaves are fairly large for an ericaceous plant varying from 1 to 3 cm (to $1\frac{1}{4}$ in) long and to 6 mm ($\frac{1}{4}$ in) wide. The upper surface is netted and dark green with narrowly revolute edges which border the grey underside with its prominent mid-vien.

There are up to 6 or 7 flowers in a tufted cluster, each on a slender stalk subtended by a small bract. A tiny 5-pointed pink calyx seems almost lost beneath the large oval-rounded corolla, also 5-partite, the points being tiny and reflexed around the narrow throat. Inside the corolla 10 horned stamens encircle the style which later persists above the dry brown capsule with its numerous seeds.

Points of Interest Carl Linnaeus was so enchanted with the flowers of this plant when he first found it on his memorable journey through Lapland that he called it *Andromeda* in memory of the beautiful Greek maiden of that name.* According to legend she was chained naked to a rock in the sea and left to be devoured by a fearsome monster to appease the god Neptune who had inflicted the monster on the country at the persuasion of his daughters who were jealous of her beauty. Fortunately for the helpless Andromeda she was rescued in time by the hero Perseus, who hid his face with his shield to save her from embarrassment. Even so, she hung her head and blushed deeply pink, the lovely colour of the flowers of the plant with its feet (roots) in water, as hers were, and which in Lapland was surrounded by toads and frogs in lieu of great sea monsters.

*See *Linnaea borealis* on page 56.

Dwarf Cornel *Cornus suecica*
Family: Cornaceae

Habitat Damp moors and heaths, mainly in mountains. Calcifuge.

Distribution Locally common in north-west Scotland between 300 and 900 m (1000 and 3000 ft). Rare in a few localities in southern Scotland and northern England. In Europe, north of 53° latitude, reaches 1200 m (4000 ft), often abundant on mountain moors.

Flowering-time June to August.

Description Surrounded by low leafy shrubs of cloudberry, bilberry and heathers amongst the squelchy black peat of northern moorlands the wide white flowerheads of these enchanting little plants supply a complete and unexpected contrast. Although these flower heads are just over 2 cm (less than 1 in) across, their milky whiteness is so pronounced that a group of plants as in the photograph seems akin to a brilliant galaxy of stars in a dark sky, and the farther north one travels the larger and more intense do the galaxies become. Not white alone but there is a second contrast in the tiny inky blue real flowers nestling in the centre of white, and all held above an array of fresh leaves, ensuring that the colony is conspicuous amongst the widening darker background.

The flower heads appear in groups because several stems arise from each main rhizome which lies buried in moss and peat. The aerial stems are from 10 to 15 cm (4 to 6 in) tall each with about 5 pairs of rounded-oval pointed leaves of which the lowest are much the smallest. Most are sessile, although the upper ones may be shortly stalked; they are bright green with 5 or 7 well-marked veins.

At the top of each flowering stem is a single inflorescence; its 4 eye-catching white parts are not petals but bracts modified to attract bees and flies for pollination. The true flowers, from 8 to 25 in number, are very small and of an unusual shade of dark purplish blue, and form a tight cluster in the centre. A hand-lens is necessary to see and identify the component parts of each perfect little flower; the small hairy calyx-tube, 4 tiny dark petals, 4 paler stamens with protruding white anthers and a projecting stigma.

After pollination a brilliant cluster of red berry-like fruits appears, the fleshy part enclosing a hard stone; some are just beginning to develop in our photograph. When ripe these attract birds which disperse the stones after eating the pulp. Although not poisonous, the fruits have no claim to flavour.

Points of Interest The only two widespread European representatives of the family Cornaceae, *Cornus suecica* and *C. sanguinea* (Dogwood) are so different in habitat, form and floral appearance that a brief comparison is worth noting. Dogwood is a small tree of limey soils, with creamy flowers in loose clusters and without bracts, followed by black fruits. But its seedlings in spring, then 10 to 15 cm (4 to 6 in) tall, are almost identical with non-flowering shoots of cornel both having fresh green leaves of the same size, shape and numbers. *C. suecica* is considered to be a highly advanced species of herb descended from woody ancestors.

Clustered Bellflower *Campanula glomerata*
Family: Campanulaceae

Habitat Meadows, roadsides, grassy places, always calcareous.

Distribution In the British Isles on dry limestone hillsides, chalk downs, and cliffs, widespread in England; a few outlying colonies in eastern Scotland and South Wales. Also found in most of the Continent from the plains to 1500 m (5000 ft), locally common.

Flowering-time July to September.

Description When walking over England's chalk downland in summer it is delightful to see amongst the short dry grass a scattering of single very dark blue 'bells' pointing skyward from leafy stems scarcely 5 cm (2 in) tall. In sharp contrast rich subalpine meadows of Europe include with their brilliant floral display tight clusters of the same dark 'bells', but up to 20 together on sturdy stems 30 cm (12 in) or more high and competing successfully with the varied and crowded multitude of colourful plants surrounding them. Though apparently so different, these 'bells' both belong to the same species *C. glomerata* which produces plants of all sizes and flowers of any number between these two extremes. With such ability to adapt its growth to its surroundings, there is little wonder at the variety of its habitat.

A sturdy hairy perennial, the main stem, of whatever height, is erect, stiff, leafy and unbranched except for short dense lateral flower clusters on the bigger specimens. These grow in the axils of the upper leaves which are sessile. The basal leaves are long-stalked and fairly broad, the stem-leaves narrower, pointed and finely toothed. Their dark green colour is softened throughout by a downy covering of short white hairs.

The outstanding characteristic of this species and the origin of its specific name *glomerata*, is the arrangement of the flowers in dense sessile clusters surrounded by leafy bracts. This, along with their unusually rich shade of dark purple-blue ensures that they are easily observed amongst other vegetation. The bells which face upward and outward (not pendent as in most large campanulas) are from 1.5 to 3 cm ($\frac{1}{2}$ to $1\frac{1}{4}$ in) long, and have each a pale green tubular calyx with 5 acuminate lobes. The 5 points of the corolla are wide and reflexed, displaying first 5 ripe mature stamens, and later a long creamy-white style and its 3 stigmas. As with other campanulas this timing leads to cross-pollination (see *C. latifolia* page 49).

Points of Interest Many plants vary in size according to situation but *C. glomerata* is undoubtedly one of the most confusing in this respect. The small few-flowered ones are sometimes mistaken for gentians even in England where blue gentians are rare and confined to a few specialised localities. For help in identification note that the leaves of the *campanula* are hairy and arranged alternately on the stem; those of gentians are smooth and in pairs. The chalk-loving gentians possess smaller flowers (except *Gentianella germanica*, page 105) which are purple and always with conspicuous white hairs at the throat of the corolla, whereas the campanula 'bell' is clear.

Pyrenean Bellflower *Campanula speciosa*
Family: Campanulaceae

Habitat On calcareous soils; scree, stony places, open sunny positions.

Distribution Endemic to south west Europe; only in France and Spain; the Cévennes, Corbières and the central and eastern Pyrenees.

Flowering-time May to July.

Description No cultivated Campanula could be more spectacularly beautiful than this; indeed the name *speciosa* meaning showy or handsome was never more suitably applied. The plants grow sparingly on steep limestone hillsides where stones and scree are tenuously bound by the roots of occasional small trees and shrubs and wiry grasses. Here where the sun warms the ground a few isolated plants flaunt a display of large bell-flowers of the richest and most glorious blue in brilliant contrast to and sheer defiance of their unstable and inhospitable terrain. All wild campanulas are beautiful; this one is magnificent.

The species is not dissimilar to the old garden favourite the Canterbury Bell *C. medium*. Like that plant it is bushy in habit, up to 60 cm (2 ft) tall and covered at flowering-time with large blue 'bells'. A stout rhizome helps to combat the shifting scree, and from it grows a basal rosette of long narrow leaves from 5 to 10 cm (2 to 4 in) and a strong erect stem, all greyish with short hairs.

The flowers which are borne singly on long slender stalks cover the plants almost to ground-level and are held horizontally to erect as seen in the photograph. Each intensely blue corolla tube is encircled at the base by a 10-lobed calyx, 5 small lobes alternating with 5 long pointed ones. The corolla itself is from 3 to 4 cm (1 to 1½ in) long and rather more than half as wide with 5 recurved petal-lobes. Within the tube are 5 stamens and a slender style with 3 stigmas; the pollination mechanism is as described for *C. latifolia* (page 49).

Points of Interest The 10-lobed calyx is useful in the identification of *C. speciosa* as most other European species have a calyx with 5 lobes only. *C. barbata*, widespread in alpine meadows, has 10, but there the small lobes are frequently black-edged. Also the plant is only about 15 to 20 cm (6 to 8 in) tall, not bushy, and the flowers, from 2 to 8 on a single stem are pendent and of a much paler porcelain blue. The few remaining species with a 10-lobed calyx are rare and local, mostly in the Balkan Peninsula and do not overlap with *C. speciosa*.

Campanula speciosa, like *Primula scotica* (page 11), is endemic to a small corner of the world, in this case the limestone hills of southern France and eastern Spain. Because of this restricted distribution it behoves those who know its locations to leave the plants unharmed, so that they remain a source, not only of great joy, but of scientific, geographical and historical interest to other people now and in the future.

Viper's-bugloss *Echium vulgare*
Family: Boraginaceae

Habitat Dry places, chalk downs, sand-dunes, roadsides, waste ground. Sea-level to subalpine.

Distribution Local eastern and southern England and Wales; occasional in Scotland and Ireland. Throughout Europe, widespread and fairly common. Usually found on calcareous soil.

Flowering-time June to September.

Description The Borage family includes many a beautiful plant of which Viper's Bugloss is one of the most strikingly handsome. Against a background of white chalk or on a bare patch of blown sand its tall blue flower-spikes provide a vivid contrast, and areas of waste land are transformed by its brilliance. Although not found everywhere, it is locally common enough to colour long stretches of roadside, large patches of shingle, and other infertile land.

It is biennial, producing in the first year only a ground rosette of leaves, dull green in colour, fairly narrow, very hairy and up to 15 cm (6 in) long. The second year sees the full plant, usually with so many spreading leafy branches that it has a shrubby appearance, especially as the stems are thick and covered with short stiff bristly hairs. The plants vary in height up to 1 m (3 ft) of which at least the upper half is thick with short side-branches bearing from 8 to 12 flowers on the upper side of a tight-curving cluster. Each side-branch grows from the axil of a hairy dark green leaf and the flowers are subtended by smaller leaflike bracts.

The flowers bloom in sequence from the lowest upward, only 3 or 4 fully open together; the unfolding buds display a rich pink colour which changes to vivid dark blue in the mature flowers, becoming purple as they wither. Thus the whole plant maintains a long flowering season through which an exciting colour variation is displayed.

Each flower has 5 pointed hairy sepals about half the length of the corolla which is 1.5 to 2 cm ($\frac{3}{4}$ in) long and composed of 5 petals united into a funnel-like tube. This is slightly 2-lipped, the upper longer lip in the form of an arched hood, while the lower is more flat and spreading. Four red stamens protrude from the corolla (inside is another shorter one) and a pale pink style ends in 2 stigmas projecting even beyond the stamens.

Points of Interest *Echium* is from the Greek word for viper and most languages incorporate a snake in the plant's local name. It is not clear as to whether the reference is due to a supposed resemblance to a snake's head and tongue by the open flower and protruding stigmas or to the recommendation by the Greek physician Dioscorides of the use of an infusion from the plant as an antidote to the bite of a snake.

The bristly leaves give rise to the English 'bugloss', also from the Greek, meaning the tongue of an ox.

Knapweed Broomrape *Orobanche elatior*
Family: Orobanchaceae

Habitat Calcareous ground.
Distribution On the chalk of eastern and southern England following its host plant; rare. Most of western and central Europe from Spain to Greece.
Flowering-time June and July.
Description The broomrapes constitute a small group of parasitic plants all with very similar colouring and characteristics, but each species with a preference for a particular type of host-plant. As this one (at least in England) is found in conjunction with the large Knapweed, *Centaurea scabiosa*, it is possible to find a colourful colony of plants, the quiet shade of the parasite offset by the bright purple feathery-tufted flowers of the Knapweed. Such a colony was ours; the 3 plants photographed were only a small part of a large group outlined against the sky when the late afternoon sunshine of summer caught the dignified yellow spikes with a beautiful glint of gold.

These stiff erect stems are brownish-yellow as are the scales which clothe them and which replace normal green leaves. The individually attractive flowers are sessile and packed fairly tightly in a long spike and each subtended by a 3-pointed hairy yellowish bract. The tubular flowers are quite large, from 18 to 25 mm (about 1 in) long, 2-lipped with crisply wavy edges and of a tawny yellow tinged with purple. The tube is evenly and gracefully arched, and beneath the upper 2-lobed lip are 4 pale brown stamens and a bright yellow 2-lobed stigma.

This Broomrape's host-plant is the most handsome of the purple-flowered Knapweeds, *Centaurea scabiosa* as in the photograph, which is widespread and often abundant on calcareous roadsides and rough grassland. About 60 cm (2 ft) tall, branched, leafy and many flowered, they can usually be identified by their large leaves which are deeply and unevenly lobed. The delicately beautiful flowers reach 7 cm (3 in) across, and are graced with an outer circlet of spreading feathery sterile florets surrounding a centre of perfect ones – that is, they possess both stamens and stigmas.

Points of Interest *Orobanche elatior* is our third plant in this book which possesses no chlorophyll and therefore no green colour. Like *Limodorum abortivum* (page 55) and *Corallorhiza trifida* (page 65), it cannot manufacture food, but in this case it is completely parasitic, being absolutely dependent upon its living host for all its food. This it obtains directly from the host's roots to which it becomes attached whilst still a seedling. All *Orobanches* produce large quantities of small dust-like seeds to ensure that sufficient of them fall to the ground within reach of the roots of the right host-plant and thus provide for the parasite's survival.

The name *Orobanche* originates from two Greek words, *Orobus*, a vetch (a plant of the family Leguminosae) and 'to strangle' and the English 'Broomrape' has a similar interpretation. Broom is also a leguminous plant, this family providing several hosts for the more common *Orobanche rapum-genistae* (Greater Broomrape).

94

Monkey Orchid *Orchis simia*
Family: Orchidaceae

Habitat Grassland, open woods, scrub: usually calcareous.
Distribution South east England only. Very rare and strictly protected. Widespread in Europe, but not common in central and southern countries.
Flowering-time April to June.
Description Monkey orchids are gay little plants. They hang out their quaint pink-purple flowers from a compact rounded head so that they really do appear like small long-legged animals swinging happily from a miniature tree. Their colouring is soft and pretty and their form and arrangement produce an orderly shagginess which is both attractive and distinctive and a guide to identification in their grassy home. Though extremely rare in England their colonies in Europe vary from a few to as many as 50 plants.

The height of the smooth light green stems varies from about 15 to 40 cm (6 to 16 in). Three or 4 broad leaves clasp the lower stem and there are 2 or 3 very small ones higher up. All are shining, never spotted, and the large ones range between 5 and 18 cm (2 and 7 in) long.

Twenty or more flowers pack the fairly dense spikes which are about 4 cm ($1\frac{1}{2}$ in) long, each flower with its own pink-tinged bract, which is shorter than the ovary. All sepals and petals except the lip converge into an erect pointed protective hood – the monkey's 'head' – silvery pink streaked with violet. The lip is irregularly divided into 2 narrow horizontal side-lobes – the 'arms' – and a central pendent lobe which is further cut into 2 outer upcurled 'legs' and a short pointed 'tail'. Again, the colour is basically pink but dark spots on white are often found on the upper lip. Altogether a delightful combination of shapes, patterns and colours; very rarely pure white flowers occur.

Points of Interest The flowers of the spikes of *O. simia* open from the top downward, a most unusual arrangement. *Orchis*, the genus from which the whole orchid family is named, is one of the largest and most important of the European members of this family. Being slow-growing plants with a highly advanced flower structure, orchids need special organs for food storage which take the form of underground tubers. Those of the genus *Orchis* are always 2 in number and oval in shape. The flowers are usually small in more or less dense spikes and each with a typical hood or helmet as here in *O. simia*. Their most characteristic colour in Europe is a variation of pink, purple and white although a few yellow species occur chiefly in Mediterranean regions.

The outwardly similar genus *Dactylorhiza* containing the handsome but puzzling marsh and spotted orchids, has now been separated from *Orchis* chiefly because its tubers are palmately lobed, and is therefore named from *dactylos*, the Greek word for a finger.

Lady Orchid *Orchis purpurea*
Family: Orchidaceae

Habitat Grassland, woodland, roadsides, on calcareous soil.
Distribution South east England only and very rare, though widespread throughout central and southern Europe. Rare and protected in Switzerland.
Flowering-time April to June.
Description As a plant *O. purpurea* is tall, strong and dignified but the individual flowers resemble charmingly dressed puppet ladies circling around a central column. It is one of the most distinctive of all the *Orchis* species, at first because of the very dark maroon-red appearance of the dense spikes in bud. Later, as these buds unfold, lower ones first, and the spikes lengthen, the pattern of alternating wine-coloured hoods and pale frilly petticoats of the ladies produces a beautiful evenly designed mosaic that even from a distance betrays the plant's identity in a most unusual and attractive way.

These are tall plants from 25 to 40 cm (10 to 16 in), occasionally even more, with strong erect stems and from 6 to 10 broad shining unspotted leaves reaching 20 cm long. The lower larger leaves are outspreading while a few smaller ones sheathe the upper stem.

The conspicuous and beautiful inflorescence is densely packed at first with very dark blackish-red buds which open gradually into an elegant flowering spike up to 10 cm (4 in) long. A small violet bract subtends each flower and the twisted ovary is about twice the length of the downward curving spur. The ladies' hoods are each formed from 3 broad sepals and 2 narrow petals folded upwards. The third petal or lip is large by comparison and is wide and slightly frilled with 2 upper small lobes and a large lower one with a central notch in which is a tiny point.

This, together with the reproductive organs, constitutes the basic flower plan for all *Orchis* species but the special charm of the Lady Orchid lies in the characteristic alternating pattern of the exceptionally dark 'hoods' and the dainty spreading 'skirts' with their scattering of raised violet-purple markings on a pale pink background. The only rival to *O. purpurea* in this respect is *O. ustulata* the Burnt Orchid, which is so much smaller in all its parts that confusion in identification is unlikely ever to arise.

Points of Interest The old name for this genus was *Satyrium* from the Greek mythical woodland gods or Satyrs who were supposed to eat the orchid tubers as an aphrodisiac. Whatever the truth of this, the tubers of some species, notably the widespread Early Purple Orchid *O. mascula* seem definitely to have yielded a substance, known as Salep or Salop, which had great value especially in times of famine. According to the herbalist Culpeper it 'will support the system in privation . . . and is good for those who are compelled to endure exposure without food'. What a good thing for the continuance of Europe's wild orchids that we now have other supplies of sustaining nourishment!

Red Helleborine *Cephalanthera rubra*
Family: Orchidaceae

Habitat Wooded areas, especially beech, bushy places, from sea-level to 1800 m (6000 ft) usually on calcareous soils.

Distribution In Britain, only very rare in southern England and protected by law in 1975. Widespread on the Continent but local, especially in central Europe. Rare and protected in Switzerland.

Flowering-time May to July.

Description Graceful slender stems and red flowers of a shade indescribable contrast beautifully with the hard light-coloured limestone scree on which these rare helleborines grow, with little apparent means of sustenance and a very tenuous foothold beneath the loose grey stones. But the plants are never far from some source of shade such as that provided by young beeches, small hazels, and bushy scrub so that throughout their summer flowering they benefit from sun and shade alternately. It is fascinating also to see how the rich flower colour appears to change from lilac-pink in full sunlight to dark rosy-red in the late evening shade.

The tallest plants may reach 60 cm (2 ft) but the average is nearer to half that height. The stem carries a few widely-spaced leaves, all rather narrow, long and pointed, their form enhancing the gracefulness of the plant, very different from the stiff carriage of the white *Cephalantheras*.

C. rubra is quite unmistakable because of the extravagantly pink flowers which resemble those of some tropical orchids on a much smaller scale. They are about $2\frac{1}{2}$ cm (1 in) across with the 6 segments almost equal in size, quite sharply pointed and as with many helleborines not always wide open. The lip is fairly broad above, strongly ridged with bright yellow, and is suddenly narrowed below into a long tapering point. It is perhaps the sharp contrast of yellow with the flower's vivid pink together with the unusual lip which lifts this species above its relatives in exotic appearance.

The flowers number from about 3 to 10 in a loose spike, their subtending green bracts being much longer than the ovaries which are downy with soft hairs.

Points of Interest This is our third Helleborine, the name being given to 2 distinct though allied genera, of the family *Orchidaceae*. The *Cephalantheras* (see also *C. longifolia*, page 53) can be distinguished from the genus *Epipactis* (see *E. palustris*, page 73) by the mode of growth of the individual flowers on the main stem. The first are sessile, each flower set upon its green twisted ovary, the second have a straight ovary, and in addition a short curving stalk which keeps the flower in a semi-drooping position.

The flowers of the *Cephalantheras* are distinctly white or pink, the *Epipactis* species display variable assortments of soft greens, reds, and pinks, with the beautiful exception of *E. palustris* already described.

Lizard Orchid *Himantoglossum hircinum*
Family: Orchidaceae

Habitat Grassy rocky places, dry banks, margins of woodland and thickets, on calcareous soils.

Distribution In the British Isles, mostly across the south-eastern half of England; rare and erratic in appearance. Local and uncommon through central and southern Europe.

Flowering-time May to July.

Description Peculiarity is the hallmark of *H. hircinum*. The tall strong plants could never be mistaken for any other when in bloom for the pink-tinged green flowers dangle from a long spike in an entanglement of curled twisted straps and laces as though nature had set out to see how crazily eccentric she could be. They are the comedians of the European orchid stage, and amongst the bevy of beauty of the principals and chorus they provide a refreshing cause for laughter – but also a source of thoughtful interest and wonderment.

This orchid is one of Europe's largest plants with pale green stems up to 90 cm (3 ft) in height and with several wide floppy leaves, about 20 cm (8 in) long. These are also pale green and unspotted, the lower ones blunt – though sometimes withering by flowering-time – the upper narrower, pointed and clasping the stem.

There can be as many as 15 to 80 flowers on the long cylindrical spike 15 cm (6 in) and though so strange they do have some claim to beauty seen through a hand-lens, especially on the extended lip. An incurved hood is formed by the smaller more regular sepals and petals, grey-green streaked with red. A short conical spur points downward behind each flower, which is sessile, and the narrow subtending bract is equal to or slightly longer than the twisted stalk-like ovary.

The lip is a fascinating structure. In bud it lies neatly coiled like a living watch-spring and as the flower opens the lip unwinds into a narrow twisted strap 4 to 5 cm ($1\frac{1}{2}$ to 2 in) long and with 2 short curled lateral lobes. As these straps swing from the spike at almost all angles, though mostly pendent, the result is often a restrained shagginess and a really good specimen in full flower can be dramatically handsome. The whole lip is a variable pattern of green and brown, plain and streaky, and distinctly red-spotted at the wider end.

Points of Interest These plants are reputed to emit a strong smell of goats, thus giving rise to an assortment of names including the specific *hircinum* from the Latin *hircus*, he-goat. *Himantoglossum* is compounded from two Greek words meaning 'a leather strap' and 'a tongue'. Many national names incorporate a mixture of these, for example the German *Bocks-Riemenzunge* comes from *Bock* (goat), *Riemen* (strap) and *Zunge* (tongue). Swedish and Dutch names are similar and the Danish *Stinkende båndtunge* is most expressive! The English 'lizard' refers to that animal's long tongue as it shoots out for food, and the French state simply and succinctly *Orchis bouc* (goat).

Chiltern Gentian *Gentianella germanica*
Family: Gentianaceae

Habitat Calcareous grassland, often on recently disturbed ground.
Distribution Only rarely in central southern England in Britain. Local but sometimes abundant in central Europe.
Flowering-time August to October.
Description Most members of this genus have purple flowers, not the brilliant blue usually associated with gentians, but they are nevertheless extremely attractive and this, one of the largest, especially so. While a few species of plants are still bravely defying the onset of autumn in the lower mountains and chalk hills it is most cheering to find the large bluish-purple silky-haired flowers of the Chiltern gentians shining in the slanting sunshine of September or even October. On the European mainland they may sometimes be found in dense clusters starring the grass for several metres, like bridesmaids' posies neatly and specially planned and planted.

The plants vary in height from 10 to 25 cm (4 to 10 in) with erect slender stems, purplish-green and usually much branched and leafy. The dark green leaves are paired, broadest near the base, and tapering gradually to a point. In their axils grow the flowers 3.5 cm (1.5 in) long, the terminal ones of each branch opening first, soft purple with a bluish tinge. The outer lower half of the flower-tube may be paler or a creamy-yellow, surrounded by the tubular calyx, greenish purple and with 5 pointed lobes, often slightly unequal in width. The corolla tube divides also into 5 (occasionally 4) spreading broadly-pointed petals, thus producing the starlike effect reminiscent of most gentians. Within the throat of the flowers is a dense fringe of long fine hairs, purple above and paler below, and it is this characteristic circlet of hairs which readily distinguishes *Gentianella* from the genus *Gentiana*.

Just inside the corolla's throat can also be seen the anthers of the 5 stamens, and 2 outspread stigmas below which is a long narrow short-stalked ovary. After pollination, usually by humble bees, this becomes a dry capsule containing numerous small seeds, later ejected when the capsule splits open.

Points of Interest *Gentianella* are separated from the genus *Gentiana* because of certain characteristic features, the most obvious being the corolla hairs as already described. *Gentiana* species possess small lobes between the petals, absent in *Gentianella*. Of the European species of *Gentianella*, *G. germanica* is the largest and is late flowering like *G. amarella* or Felwort, the one most easily confused with it. Though usually smaller, *G. amarella* is variable in size, from 2.5 cm (1 in) to 25 cm (10 in) tall, but the flowers are always small, 10 to 15 mm, and much darker in colour. It is more widespread as is *G. campestris*, Field Gentian which can be distinguished by having 4 petals and 4 sepals, of which the 2 inner ones are narrow and pointed, and the 2 outer ones much wider and overlapping the former.

Occasionally, white flowering forms of gentianellas occur but we have not seen or heard of these in *G. germanica*.

Christmas Rose *Helleborus niger*
Family: Ranunculaceae

Habitat Subalpine woods and shady mountain slopes to 1850 m (6000 ft) on calcareous soil.
Distribution Central and Eastern Alps, Carpathians, Northern Apennines. Protected in Switzerland. Not British except in gardens.
Flowering-time December to May depending upon altitude.
Description So familiar must be the image of these evocative flowers from Christmas cards, floral decorations and calendars that it seems hardly necessary to describe them. But none of these can compare with the clear beauty of the plants themselves in their mountain home, living as they do at the snow's cold margin and uplifting their wide-open white flowers to the pale glint of wintry sunlight. White-capped peaks in the distance, leafless larches and dark pines around them, the contrasting picture of exquisite beauty is literally breath-taking.

The drooping white buds break through the wet soil before their stalks are visible, a habit found in other early-flowering mountain plants. Gradually the stalks lengthen to a height of 8 to 15 cm (3 to 6 in) and the buds, usually single, become horizontal before opening to display the flat wide flowers about 5 cm (2 in) across. The 5 white conspicuous parts are sepals, a feature of many members of *Ranunculaceae*. Inside these are a few small greenish tubular petals modified into nectar-containing organs which attract insects to effect cross-pollination.

The flower-centre is bright with numerous yellow anthers on long white filaments and through them a few green styles thrust the ripening stigmas. After pollination the white sepals turn green, sometimes flushed pink or white and persist thus for some weeks as the central pistils swell into large green pod-like seedheads.

New leaves appear direct from the rootstock during or just after flowering and are shining bright green and divided into about 9 leathery uneven leaflets, 8 to 12 cm (3 to 5 in) long. They remain through the year and may be found buried beneath the snow around the next generation of opening flowers.

Points of Interest The lovely name Christmas Rose is an obvious choice for rose-like flowers in bloom during the Christmas season. However, the flower's structure is not that of a true rose, although some features of *Rosaceae* and *Ranunculaceae* are superficially similar, especially the wide flowers and numerous stamens and carpels.

The specific name *niger* means black and the reason for this lies hidden beneath the ground in the form of highly poisonous black fibrous roots. Although a few writers indicate possible curative properties, especially against madness they are mostly indefinite about the plants' virtues whereas their properties as a poisonous emetic are stated very strongly.

For the non-medical person, therefore, it seems best simply to enjoy the plants for their glorious winter-cheering grace and charm as nothing can excel their exquisite beauty as they push through the virgin snow.

Spring Anemone · *Pulsatilla vernalis*
Family: Ranunculaceae

Habitat Subarctic-alpine. Mountain pastures and meadows, moraine margins and glacier valleys, wet gullies, flowering immediately after the melting snow; from 1300 to 2750 m (4000 to 9000 ft). In its northerly stations it grows in more lowland areas, including light coniferous woodland; reaches 1860 m (6000 ft) in Norway.

Distribution Throughout much of Europe especially Northern and Central, in the above situations. Not found in the British Isles.

Flowering-time April to July; at its best in early spring.

Description The spring display of this most beautiful plant is one of the greatest delights offered by the European mountains to the alpine wanderer. The wet stony hillsides, especially the higher mounds are dappled with countless thousands of large silky opalescent flowers, betwixt gullies and hollows, still deep in the snow of winter. The contrast between the delicate lilac sheen of the flowers' dancing heads, the cold glistening snow, and the stark backdrop of towering white mountains is a never-to-be-forgotten experience of wondrous beauty.

As the snow melts from the pastures and beside the streams the flower-buds, thick with bronze-gold hairs, appear singly, held erect on sturdy short stems of only 15 mm ($\frac{2}{3}$ in). Those in our picture show a later stage in their development with the flowers, still closed, beginning

to expand and show their colouring through the soft hairs. They were photographed during a sharp shower of hail which left them delightfully enhanced by sparkling crystal droplets.

Pulsatillas are flowers of relatively simple structure; the large coloured parts replace sepals and petals, stamens and carpels are many, and each flower is followed by a feathery fruiting-head of numerous single seeds with long hairy plumes thus ensuring wind-dispersal. As these fruits form the finely-cut bracts and leaves develop and the stalk lengthens, so that the fruiting-plant can be as much as 25 cm (10 in) tall. By that time the seedheads are drooping, the sepals are papery, golden-brown and persistent for some time, and thus, after the flowers' fading, the plants are still beautiful.

When fully open the flowers are 5 to 7 cm across, smooth and pearly white inside, softly hairy and delicately suffused with lilac or pale pink outside. The plants are hairy, especially stems, bracts and buds, but less so than *Pulsatilla halleri* (page 111) and the hairs are golden, whereas those of *P. halleri* are silvery. The leaves are green, broadly-lobed and persistent through the winter, all these factors distinguishing *P. vernalis* from *P. halleri*.

Points of Interest The name *Pulsatilla* given by the great Swedish botanist Linnaeus, means 'beaten about', in this case, by the wind. The plants used to be grouped with the genus *Anemone* (from the Greek 'daughter of the wind') but have recently been separated, the most obvious difference being in the seed-heads. Those of the genus *Anemone* have a tight head of hard green seeds, without plumes.

Haller's Anemone *Pulsatilla halleri*
Family: Ranunculaceae

Habitat Dry stony pastures in mountains from 1000 to 2500 m (3500 to 8000 ft).

Distribution Widely distributed in Europe, but the colonies are local and isolated and are apparently relict populations which have developed slightly differently from one another giving rise to a number of subspecies. Our photograph shows *Pulsatilla halleri* subsp. *halleri* which is found locally in the southwest and central Alps. Not British.

Flowering-time May to July.

Description Amongst the most strikingly beautiful of European plants the purple pulsatillas must rank with the highest. *Pulsatilla halleri* is one of the most rare and local of these and fortunate indeed is he who discovers a colony when their large flowers of rich violet are in full bloom on a boulder-strewn steep hillside. Sometimes sheltered by the sombre green shoots of dwarf juniper, sometimes scattered sparingly amongst loose grey stones, or nestling securely in clusters at the base of a large inhospitable rock, these wonderful plants always present a picture of delicate loveliness which belies their strength to survive such windswept situations but which nonetheless is in harmony with the surrounding mountain landscape.

At flowering time the stems are short, from 5 to 15 cm (2 to 6 in), and each carries one large flower with from 5 to 8 spreading petal-like sepals 3 to 4 cm (about $1\frac{1}{2}$ in) long and of a beautiful violet-purple colour, darker in bud, becoming paler in older flowers. The centre is thick with numerous yellow stamens and slightly feathered carpels; the latter develop into a head of long beautifully-plumed seeds as seen in the photograph and these are individually dispersed by the wind. By this time the flowering stem has considerably lengthened.

The leaves emerge with the flowers and are finely-cut into several very narrow pointed lobes, as are the similar stalkless bracts which encircle the stem below the flower. The whole plant except the inside of the flower is so densely clothed with short silvery silky hairs that the green of the leaves is almost masked, and the already beautiful texture and colouring of the sepals are greatly enhanced.

Points of Interest *Pulsatilla halleri* is closely related to *P. vulgaris*, the Pasqueflower (Easter Flower) of England and western, central and northern Europe. This plant flowers earlier in the year as its English name implies and was formerly gathered for decoration of the Churches at Easter. Although this is a happy idea it is a malpractice; the plants are now so rare in England mainly due to the ploughing of the chalk downland where they grow, and also far from common in Europe, that they should now be left untouched to flower and seed and recover their much reduced numbers. The flowers are of an exceptionally dark purple, a truly royal colour, against which the bright stamens glow with equally royal gold.

Yellow Alpine Anemone *Pulsatilla alpina* subsp. *apiifolia*
Family: Ranunculaceae

Habitat Alpine and subalpine. Mountain meadows and pastures on primary rock, from 1 000 to 2800 m (4000 to 9000 ft).

Distribution Mountains of central and southern Europe. Widespread, but not British.

Flowering-time June to August, depending upon situation and altitude.

Description These tall handsome anemones of summer provide one of the gayest of pictures when the stony hillside pastures are thronged with their large sulphur-yellow flowers proudly uplifted to the sky. Thousands of them wave in the wind, as in our photograph, often dominating the scene and dwarfing all smaller plants. On a bright sunny day they reflect the atmosphere of warmth and light characteristic of the long days of the mountain summer. But if we travel higher and away from friendly valleys, the clusters of plants become smaller and more scattered, the surroundings wilder and more remote, and there the subtle yellow of the flowers contrasts beautifully with the hard coldness of glaciers and snow-filled gullies.

The buds of these plants are visible in May when their relative *Pulsatilla vernalis* is already in flower. They are furry with hairs of a lovely soft purple-grey and held aloft on stems from 5 to 15 cm (2 to 6 in) tall, and the surrounding frill of bracts is already in evidence. The stems are reddish and like the buds, covered with fine purple-grey hairs. Later, when the flowers are open these plants are the tallest and most sturdy of the Pulsatillas reaching a height of from 10 to 50 cm (4 to 20 in) according to altitude and situation. Like many of this genus the whole

plant is hairy but much less so than the two already described, *P. vernalis* and *P. halleri* perhaps because the Alpine Pulsatillas bloom later when the winds are less cold and their precious water-supply less precarious.

The stems are ringed with leafy bracts, in this species long-stalked and well below the flowers. The basal leaves are large, green with long stalks and finely-divided giving a densely fernlike appearance to the plants.

Each flower consists of 6 yellow petal-like parts, broad with rounded points, and 2 to 4 cm ($\frac{3}{4}$ to $1\frac{1}{2}$ in) long, one of the largest flowers in the alpine flora. Later comes the typical feathered seedhead, also large with plumes each about 4 cm ($1\frac{1}{2}$ in) long; then the hillside becomes a sea of nodding shimmering waves of silvery-pink – until the wind scatters the seeds far and wide ready to create new growth and life.

Points of Interest The seedheads have given rise to a variety of local names, a typical one being the German *Petersbart* (Peter's beard). 'Shock-headed Peter' is another one, both, no doubt, referring to the saint of that name.

The name *Pulsatilla alpina* is given to a similar plant with white flowers, delicately shading to pale blue on the outside. The yellow-flowered form here described is now given the status of a subspecies, *P. alpina* subsp. *apiifolia*. Over the years much confusion has arisen by the frequent changing of the scientific name of this subspecies. Both types flower at the same time and are much alike in all features except flower-colour. The white form is usually smaller than the yellow, although both are variable as already indicated. Both also are widespread and often abundant but rarely do they grow together; the white one prefers a limestone foundation and the yellow likes granitic types of rock. Both are poisonous to cattle.

Mountain Avens *Dryas octopetala*
Family: Rosaceae

Habitat Arctic-alpine. Stony pastures on basic rocks on mountains from 800 to 2500 m (2500 to 8000 ft) descending to sea-level in its northerly stations.

Distribution In the British Isles, uncommon in the mountains of Scotland, very rare in those of North Wales, Northern England and south west Ireland; up to 1050 m (3250 ft). Locally abundant on cliffs almost to sea-level in north-west Scotland and on the Burren limestone of western Ireland. In Europe, widespread and locally common in mountains from the Pyrenees to the Caucasus and in the Arctic.

Flowering-time May to August depending upon altitude and latitude.

Description *Dryas octopetala* is one of the most fascinating members of the European flora. Sunny places based on limestone are the home of these beautiful spreading plants. At flowering-time their large rose-like flowers bedeck the rocks with hummocks of shining white and gold, often several square metres in extent. Any space between the flowers is filled with a dark foil of glossy oak-like leaves and the glorious picture thus provided gives the finder a memory long to be treasured. When in the company of other flowers such as blue gentians, rosy moss campion or yellow rockroses, a more enchanting sight is hard to imagine.

Alternatively, on sheer cliff-faces of their northerly situations the blossoms cascade like living waterfalls over the rocks within a framework of stark grandeur.

Dryas is a long-lived perennial with a tough rootstock from which many woody branches

spread in all directions. These are covered with evergreen leaves broadly indented and 1 to 3 cm ($\frac{1}{3}$ to 1 in) long. Their upper surface is dark glossy green and strongly veined, while beneath they are grey and felted with hairs. The flowers, about 3 to 4 cm ($1\frac{1}{4}$ to $1\frac{1}{2}$ in) across grow singly on stalks 3 to 8 cm ($1\frac{1}{4}$ to 3 in) long and possess 8 brownish hairy sepals and 8 broad white petals, hence the specific name *octopetala*. Occasionally there may be more than 8 petals and we have counted up to 24 on some Irish plants. The centres are golden with numerous stamens surrounding several green carpels, both characteristic of the rose family.

Cross-pollination is effected by bees, after which the carpels develop into delicate feathery seeds, so that the brilliant white flowering-carpets are subtly changed into coverlets of silvery-grey. When caught in the slanting sunlight of evening as in our photograph they are exquisite indeed. This is nature's way of ensuring wide dispersal of the seeds by wind.

Points of Interest The name *Dryas* means a tree-nymph, from the Greek word for oak, because of its oak-like leaves.

These beautiful plants grace many differing areas in the northern hemisphere from Siberia to the American Rocky Mountains. They thrive equally well at heights of 3000 m (10,000 ft) and at sea-level of cold northern regions. They belong to the Land of the Midnight Sun as also to Europe's high alpine pastures and Britain's Atlantic shores. There they grow now, but they also belong to the far distant past of the Ice-age some 10 to 20,000 years ago; a chapter of history current today. Research shows that *Dryas octopetala* once was a plant of southern England; remains of it and other mountain plants have been found in fossil deposits there and in lowland Europe. This exciting discovery has opened up tremendous possibilities as to the origins of our flora and the solving of many puzzling ecological and geographical problems.

Alpine Rose *Rosa pendulina*
Family: Rosaceae

Habitat Subalpine to 2600 m (8000 ft). Woods and rocky pastures.
Distribution Mountains of central and south east Europe. Not British.
Flowering-time May to August.
Description Roses are favourite flowers the world over. Wide open to the sun, their exquisite texture, attractive foliage and sweet perfume combine to enchant people of all countries in hills and lowlands alike. In the European mountains *Rosa pendulina* the true 'alpine rose'* displays flowers of rich velvet pink in sharp contrast to its small subalpine neighbours as it fills the warm summer air with its fragrance.

The plants are shrubby, up to 2 m (6½ ft) tall with bright green leaves, pinnately divided into about 9 sharply toothed leaflets. This species is exceptional in having none of the large thorns characteristic of the genus *Rosa*, but its leafstalks, leaf midribs and young shoots usually possess scattered small bristles.

Five long pointed sepals alternate with five large petals in the centre of which numerous stamens surround the clustered styles. Later the familiar bright red seed-containing hips appear, as the green receptacles beneath the flowers swell and change colour. Seed dispersal is by birds who eat the pulpy cases and disgorge their contents.

Points of Interest The fruits of *Rosa pendulina* provide a medicine helpful in cases of diarrhoea, and from the seeds excellent tea can be obtained after washing, drying and an hour's stewing.   *See *Rhododendron ferrugineum* on page 132.

Lady's Mantle *Alchemilla glabra*
Family: Rosaceae

Habitat Subalpine pastures, streamsides, rock ledges, to 2400 m (8000 ft).
Distribution Throughout most of Britain, though rare in the south east, reaching nearly 1200 m (4000 ft). Most of Europe, except extreme north and south.
Flowering-time May to September.
Description The visible attraction of most plants lies in their flowers. Here is an exception; the focal point of the *Alchemillas* is their delightful foliage, leaves so large, soft and shapely that the name Lady's Mantle is wonderfully appropriate; a cloak especially for the Virgin Mary. Often their beauty of form is marvellously enhanced by the presence of shining drops of liquid around their margins like dewy lamps lighting some dark-rimmed estate.

The genus *Alchemilla* consists of several similar species, the decisive factors being leaf-shape, degree of hairiness and flower structure. Our plant is relatively smooth with few hairs, hence the name *glabra*, and with spreading stems and large basal shallow-lobed leaves on long stalks. The flowers are yellowish-green and individually insignificant in loose stalked clusters.
Points of Interest The dewy globules around the leaf margins are exuded from the leaves themselves, a beautiful and unusual device for keeping the fluid content of the plant moving at times of high humidity of the surrounding air.

The *Alchemillas* make excellent cattle fodder and the quality of the well-known Swiss Gruyéres cheese is reputed to be largely due to the prevalence of these plants.

117

Sad Stock *Matthiola fruticulosa*
Family: Cruciferae

Habitat Rocky and gravelly places in the sun, usually calcareous.
Distribution Southern Europe from Portugal to Greece and Bulgaria. Hills and mountains to 2000 m (6500 ft); rare. Not British.
Flowering-time May to August.
Description There was nothing at all sad about the colony of this rare stock, *Matthiola fruticulosa*, which greeted us from a most unstable and inhospitable slope of limestone scree one brilliantly sunny afternoon. The plants were thriving strongly with masses of beautiful reddish-purple crinkly flowers in harmony with the soft grey-green leaves below them. All were held defiantly in position by tough woody stems twisting tortuously through and around the loose stones of their insecure home. On such a day and in such a place they were joyous to behold, a delightful example of nature's sculpture perfectly adapted to the prevailing difficult conditions.

From a perennial woody base the plants grow to a height of some 20 to 30 cm (8 to 12 in) of which the lower half is clothed with narrow leaves, grey-green due to a covering of short white hairs. Their margins are smooth or slightly broken by a few small lobes. The flowers are held in clusters above the leaves, usually sessile, occasionally with very short stalks; each flower has 4 sepals, greyish and hairy, and 4 spreading or reflexed petals in the form of a cross. These are narrow, very wavy or crinkled and variable in colour. Shades and mixtures of green, rust, pink and purple have been recorded; we found one small colony with dull brownish-pink flowers but all others in different places were the warm red-purple of the photograph. It is presumably the more sombre colours which are responsible for the plant's older name of *M. tristis* or 'sad' Stock.

A 2-lobed stigma is visible inside the corolla-tube on top of the narrow ovary for there is no style. After pollination the ovary lengthens into a very long narrow pod sometimes with a tiny horn at the top and containing numerous small hard seeds.

Points of Interest The genus *Matthiola* is named after a famous Italian Renaissance botanist and contains some of the most attractive and colourful members of the family Cruciferae. Many, like their near relatives, the *Cheiranthus* or Wallflowers, are widely cultivated for the beauty of their glowing red, pink and purple flowers and for their perfume which is rich enough to be enjoyed well beyond the massed flower-beds which they adorn.

In the wild, *M. fruticulosa* is far from common though it grows in North Africa and western parts of Asia as well as in Europe. There is a sub-species *M. fruticulosa* subsp. *valesiaca*, even more rare and local; it is an alpine European endemic.

Wild Pink *Dianthus sylvestris*
Family: Caryophyllaceae

Habitat Stony places, rocks, cliffs to 2800 m (9000 ft).
Distribution Widespread in mountains of central and southern Europe. Not British.
Flowering-time June to August.
Description Sun-loving and rock-clinging, glorious bouquets of rosy pink flowers belonging to the lovely wild *Dianthus* beckon from high cliff ledges and the steepest of stony slopes. When the sky above them is blue and the cliffs are bright with sunlight, the contrasting rich warm colour of the flowers in such an exciting setting brings to perfection the scene of a typically alpine summer's day.

Because many plants of the genus *Dianthus* like sunshine and stony places, they possess a stout taproot to hold them in their precarious situation, whilst their very narrow glaucous leaves, mostly in a basal tuft, keep evaporation of water to a minimum. The slender stems of this variable species are from 5 to 45 cm (2 to 18 in) long with a few pairs of small leaves 1 to 2 cm (less than 1 in) situated at wide intervals.

The fairly large flowers are rarely more than 3 to a plant. Each has a long 5-pointed tubular calyx with 2 small scales at the base and both surrounding the corolla tube which divides into 5 delicately fringed petals. There are 10 stamens and 3 styles which protrude when the stigmas mature. It is possible that the thick calyx tube, fortified by the scales, helps to prevent rogue insects from stealing nectar, by making it difficult for them to bite through the flower-tube.

Hacquetia *Hacquetia epipactis*
Family: Umbelliferae

Habitat Bushy shady places, woods, to 1500 m (5000 ft).
Distribution Local in the eastern Alps of Austria, Italy and Yugoslavia, also the northern Carpathians, Czechoslovakia and Poland. Not British.
Flowering-time April and May.
Description Plants with little or no colouring other than green may not be conspicuous like those with bright flowers but they often display a fascinating charm of their own. These little plants of *Hacquetia* nestle into mossy mounds and banks of leaf mould with an intense greenness rarely seen. Their colourful neighbours, including purple spring vetchlings, white anemones, periwinkle and hepaticas of two different blues form a kaleidoscopic framework around them so that each is enhanced by the presence of the others.

From a perennial creeping rhizome grow a number of long-stalked bright green leaves and simple erect leafless stems, 10 to 25 cm (4 to 10 in) and each with one umbel of tiny yellow flowers. These are crowded into a dense rounded head, scarcely 2 cm ($\frac{3}{4}$ in) across, and beautifully surrounded by a halo of leafy bracts. The large leaves are palmately divided into from 3 to 5 wedge-shaped leaflets themselves further lobed and toothed towards the apex. The 5 yellow sepals of each small flower are more conspicuous than the 5 petals, also yellow, which surround 5 stamens and 2 styles. The whole plant is thus a lovely harmony of shining yellow-green, with the latter predominating.

Large-flowered Butterwort *Pinguicula grandiflora*
Family: Lentibulariaceae

Habitat Bogs, wet meadows, wet rocks.

Distribution Only south west Ireland, north to County Clare, in the British Isles. In Europe, the mountains of northern Spain, the Pyrenees, French Alps, French and Swiss Jura. Endemic to Europe.

Flowering-time May to August.

Description Though restricted in distribution, this largest of Europe's Butterworts seems equally happy in soggy wet bogs and on sheer cliffs which are constantly subject to dripping or seeping of water from above. On such a cliff grew the plants in this photograph; on that cliff nature's liberal hand had painted a most wonderful design of soft yet glowing violet-purple and pale yellow-green – a mural of marvellous beauty. An enchanting mural alive with masses of royal flowers and fly-filled leaves all gaining sustenance from the moist humus of the liverwort-covered permanently wet rock.

The difficult habitat and unusual mode of life of the *Pinguiculas*, which are insectivorous, are reflected in the plants' structure and appearance. Roots are few and short as not much food absorption is required of them, and the fly-catching leaves, all in a basal rosette on the ground, are stalkless, large, 3 to 8 cm (1 to $3\frac{1}{2}$ in) and bright yellow-green.

Each leafless glandular stalk is crowned with a single superb flower whose corolla may be 3.5 cm (nearly $1\frac{1}{2}$ in) across. This is 2-lipped, the lower being larger with 3 petals overlapping into a wide rounded frill, its royal purple offset by a streaked white centre, and behind is a long spur containing nectar.

Points of Interest The glandular leaves present a sticky shining surface to the light which attracts small flies. These are absorbed by a digestive juice exuded by the glands and the plant in the photograph shows ample evidence of this manner of feeding.

P. grandiflora is confined in Europe to western hills and mountains except for its isolated appearance 500 to 600 miles away in South west Ireland where it is native and locally richly abundant. It is believed to be a relict species surviving there from before the time of the separation of Great Britain and Ireland from Europe and from each other, a fascinating fact of plant history, geography and distribution.

Irish Saxifrage *Saxifraga rosacea*
Family: Saxifragaceae

Habitat and Distribution Rocky places in the mountains of central Germany, western Czechoslovakia and the Vosges. From sea-level to the mountains in western Ireland. Endemic to Europe.

Flowering-time May to July.

Description Saxifrages are associated with the two extremes of rocky mountain wildness and home alpine gardening, and they rank high amongst the best known and most appreciated of all alpine plants. Our first example is a typical 'mossy' saxifrage whose small leaves are so densely crowded and finely divided that when not in bloom the plants resemble cushions of green moss. At flowering-time these are transformed into unbelievable beauty when stony slabs are covered and cracks are filled with thousands of creamy white flowers converting the bleak scene into a wonderful wild rock garden.

S. rosacea is a local plant, but sometimes abundant, usually compact with leaves and stems ranging from bright green to tawny red within the same colony. Its height is from 5 to 15 cm (2 to 6 in) with flowers up to 17 mm ($\frac{3}{4}$ in) across, the petals wide and rounded. Our photograph shows a cushion of flowers in bloom 60 cm (2 ft) across.

Points of Interest Like *Pinguicula grandiflora* (page 123), *S. rosacea* grows in two widely separated locations, the central European mountains and south west Ireland.

124

Trumpet Gentian *Gentiana acaulis* aggregate
Family: Gentianaceae

Habitat Alpine pastures from 1200 to 2700 m (3800 to 9000 ft).
Distribution Pyrenees, Alps, Northern Apennines, Jura, Cévennes, Carpathians. Not British.
Flowering-time May to August, depending upon altitude.
Description When the pastures of the Alps in summer are dappled deep dark blue with gentians there can be no floral landscape more glorious in all Europe. Posies and nosegays, blue unlike any other blue, nestle in the grass and raise their brilliant trumpets in a triumphant paean to the warmth and light of the sun on which their very existence depends.

The *acaulis* (stemless) group of gentians is subdivided into a number of species, that in the photograph being the uncommon *G. angustifolia* (narrow-leaved gentian). Superficially they are much alike; all are stemless or short-stalked perennials up to 10 cm (4 in), with a basal rosette of large smooth leaves which vary slightly in shape and texture. The 5-pointed calyx is also a deciding factor in identification; the sepal lobes may be erect or outspreading, straight-sided or indented. The two most common species are *G. clusii* with consistently dark blue unspotted flowers, on limestone formations, and *G. acaulis* itself whose flowers are usually blue, green-spotted, occasionally purplish, pale blue or greenish-white, and which prefers primary rocks. All are sensitive to warmth and light; cloudy weather keeps the flowers closed.

Wedge-leaved Saxifrage *Saxifraga cuneifolia*
Family: Saxifragaceae

Habitat Subalpine. Damp shady rocky places from 1000 to 2300 m (3300 to 7000 ft).

Distribution European mountains from the Pyrenees across to the Carpathians. Locally common. Not British.

Flowering-time June to August according to situation.

Description The saxifrages are undoubtedly the stars of the mountains. This is perhaps a lesser known European species, but it is widespread occurring locally in large numbers. Its spreading white flowers, though very small, form a delicate lacy pattern in the shadow of mossy rocks or forbidding boulders and by shaded mountain streams. Rooted in cool crevices or moist humus the plants range from 10 to 30 cm (4 to 12 in) in height, with slender leafless stems arising from basal rosettes of leaves. A peculiar characteristic of this species is the persistency of these rosettes which remain in successive whorls on the lower part of the stem and up to 5 in number. The youngest leaves are green and smooth above, purplish-brown below and slightly leathery, and they become progressively more limp and brown downwards to the lowest shrivelled ones. When fresh they are about 2 cm ($\frac{3}{4}$ in) long, slightly toothed and wedge-shaped, narrowing into a very short stalk.

The starry white flowers grow in loose clusters on the thin branched stem, and are very small, only 7 mm ($\frac{1}{4}$ in) across. Five tiny green sepals are reflexed at flowering-time and alternate with 5 narrow petals splashed with bright yellow above the base on the inner side. There are 10 stamens, 5 opposite the petals and 5 between them, characteristic of the genus. These mature at different times so that all stages may be found in one flower, from anthers thick with yellow pollen to filaments whose anthers have completely died away. A central round green ovary with 2 short styles completes a regular and comparatively simple type of flower structure.

Points of Interest About 200 species of *Saxifraga* penetrate all great mountain chains of the Northern Hemisphere to the Arctic region, and southerly through the Andes of South America to the Antartic Circle. This is a tremendous range of territory for such small plants.

The production of ground-hugging leaf-rosettes is characteristic of many saxifrages for it leads to the exclusion of other competitive species in the immediate neighbourhood. The accumulation of the rosettes as found in *S. cuneifolia* is more unusual, but will presumably assist such small plants even further in their continuous struggle for space and food.

Purple Gentian *Gentiana purpurea*
Family: Gentianaceae

Habitat Alpine and subalpine meadows and pastures from 1500 to 2600 m (5000 to 8500 ft).
Distribution Mountains of central Europe and southern Norway. Protected in France and Switzerland. Not British.
Flowering-time July and August.
Description Gentians are not always blue stars nestling amongst short turf. Some are tall, stiff and stately with red or yellow flowers thus contrasting sharply with the usual picture of these well-loved plants. Such a one is *G. purpurea*, its soft dark red flowers slightly suffused with purple and held aloft in compact clusters. These lovely purple gentians reflect the warmth and sunlight of the long summer days of their blossoming, the alpine blue sky above them and the brilliance of a multitude of lesser plants around.

Gentiana purpurea is a sturdy perennial 30 to 60 cm (1 to 2 ft) tall, glabrous and with simple erect stems each crowned with a dense inflorescence of from 5 to 10 large flowers. The lower leaves are fairly broad and shortly stalked, the upper ones narrower and sessile, about 10 cm (4 in) long and all with conspicuous veins. They are typical of gentians in their arrangement in pairs facing alternately up the stem. Five or six shorter leaflike bracts encircle the base of the topmost flower-cluster and there may be smaller groups of flowers in the axils of the upper leaves.

Each separate flower possesses a calyx peculiar to this species in the form of a papery sheathing tube slit down one side to the base. The corolla resembles an upturned bell, in all about 4 cm ($1\frac{3}{4}$ in) long with the upper quarter divided into 5 or 6 bluntly rounded lobes which are only rarely outspread in strong sunshine. Then the inner markings of yellow and green can be seen, part of the design to attract cross-pollination by insects. The arrangement for this is similar to that described for *G. pneumonanthe* (page 77); the tube of united anthers is visible within the corolla throat, and the style and 2 spreading stigmas are prominent in older flowers.

Points of Interest Many an alpine wanderer must have sampled *Enzian* or Gentian Brandy, which is obtained from *G. purpurea*, *G. punctata*, *G. pannonica* and, most frequently *G. lutea*, the most conspicuous of the group. This yellow gentian reaches 150 cm (5 ft) in height, and has thick-roots more than 90 cm (3 ft) in length. These huge roots are crushed and left to ferment, there being sufficient sugar for this purpose within the plants themselves. The resulting bitter liqueur is considered a valuable remedy for a varied assortment of complaints.

The plants used to be uprooted by nomadic 'gentian-diggers' who supplied the local herbalists with their requirements. However, *G. lutea* at least has suffered so much from this practice that it is now very rare in some of its former localities and is now on the protected list in Switzerland. In some countries it is specially cultivated for medicinal use.

Alpine Bartsia *Bartsia alpina*
Family: Scrophulariaceae

Habitat Arctic-alpine. Damp meadows, grassy places, snow-beds.

Distribution Mountains of northern England and Scotland to 900 m (3000 ft); local. All European mountains, to arctic Russia, 1100 to 2700 m (3500 to 8500 ft); locally common.

Flowering-time July to August.

Description Set amongst the brilliance of the alpine flora this small plant is far from spectacular though often abundant in damp grassy places especially those recently freed from late-lying snow. Nevertheless it possesses a quiet charm with its unusual dark purple colouring which suffuses almost completely the upper half of the plant. This sombre appearance is relieved when the shining rays of strong mountain sunlight catch with silver its coat of soft white hairs, a protective covering so necessary in this world of fast changing temperatures.

Several erect unbranched stems spring from an underground rhizome for the plants are perennial, often many together in a compact group of fairly uniform height averaging about 18 cm (7 in). These square stems are dark green below, variegated with purple above, hairy, and with about 8 pairs of sessile oval leaves. The larger ones are 2 cm ($\frac{3}{4}$ in) long and all have evenly-toothed edges, well-marked netted veins, and a covering of fine hairs. The lowest leaves are green, the others with increasing amounts of purple until the uppermost merge into purple bracts subtending the darker purple flowers, which are sessile in opposite pairs. A 5-pointed green calyx encircles the lower half of the tubular corolla which is gently arched and 2-lipped. The upper lip forms a hood slightly longer than the lower one which is hairy. Within the tube are 4 curved stamens, 2 long and 2 short, the filaments pale purple and the anthers yellowish white with hairs, just protruding from the corolla when ripe. Longer still is the purple style thus completing a saga of purple, the only slight relief provided by the attractively whiskered anthers.

Points of Interest In the year 1737 the great Swedish botanist Carl Linnaeus was offered a post as Doctor to the Dutch Trading Company in Surinam, South America. He refused partly because of his dislike of the tropical climate. He recommended instead his brilliant young German friend Johann Bartsch of Königsberg whom he had imbued with an intense love of plants. Bartsch readily agreed, hoping to investigate the tropical flora, but after arrival he suffered such ill-treatment from the Governor that after only six months' work he died. Linnaeus was greatly distressed, feeling himself responsible, and in sorrow he later named this dark-flowered plant *Bartsia (Bartschia) alpina* in his memory.

Some German flower-books give the name *Trauerblume*, Mourning Flower, for this plant of sombre colour which commemorates Germany's 'Brightest and certainly most learned ornament' as Linnaeus afterwards described him.

Alpenrose *Rhododendron ferrugineum*
Family: Ericaceae

Habitat Bouldered hillsides, mountain pastures on primary rocks.
Distribution Pyrenees, Alps, Jura, Apennines. Often abundant. Not British.
Flowering-time May to August depending on altitude.
Description Here we portray another alpine favourite ranking high in popularity with edelweiss and gentians although so different from either. In early summer the massed evergreen shrubs display dappled designs of deep pink buds like little lamps slow in lighting. Then suddenly the glory of full flowering cloaks the hillsides with glowing red as though a torch had swept the slopes kindling every bush on its way. Equally beautiful are individual plants flourishing amongst lichen-lined boulders which provide for them a moist rootrun.

The bushes attain 90 cm (3 ft) in height, woody below and with young green twigs pocked with glands above. At first the leaves are glossy green but later they darken above and become densely covered with resinous rusty-coloured glands beneath, giving the name *ferrugineum*. The leafy twigs carry loose clusters of deep rosy pink bell-like flowers with tiny green glands on the outside. Each flower has a small calyx, 5 spreading petal-lobes, 10 stamens and a pink style, half the stamens' length.

Points of Interest The leaf-glands of *R. ferrugineum* readily absorb and hold water thus preventing excessive loss of this precious commodity. On limestone this species is replaced by the similar *R. hirsutum* whose leaves are not glandular but possess instead a neat fringe of hairs along their margins, a different device with the same essential function.

Yellow Flax *Linum campanulatum*
Family: Linaceae

Habitat Dry hills, usually limestone.
Distribution Mediterranean, eastern Spain, Italy, France north to the Cèvennes. European endemic. Not British.
Flowering-time April to June, according to situation.
Description Flax is one of the oldest plants known to man but the flax fields of cultivation are beautifully blue. It can be quite a surprise therefore to discover scattered small mounds of glorious gold decorating bare crumbly soil of limestone hills and learn that they also are flax!

This species is perennial growing from a woody rootstock with clustered spreading slender stems from 5 to 25 cm (2 to 10 in) long and each carrying a few narrow leaves with whitish margins. The basal leaves are broader and spathulate. Three to 5 golden yellow flowers grow in clusters; they are delicately marked with orange veins and from 25 to 35 mm (1 to $1\frac{1}{2}$ in) wide. The 5 petals of each flower are outspread above, but they possess long claws which extend downward to give the appearance of a tubular corolla. The specific name *campanulatum* means bell-like. Five narrow pointed sepals elongate beyond the capsule after the evanescent petals have fallen.
Points of Interest The production of linen from the unusually long fibres, 60 to 90 cm (2 to 3 ft), of flax stems is recorded in Egypt from 2000 B.C. and was later brought to Europe by the Phoenicians. The seeds of cultivated blue-flowered flax produce linseed oil.

Stemless Carline Thistle *Carlina acaulis*
Family: Compositae

Habitat Dry alpine pastures, usually limestone to 2500 m (8200 ft).
Distribution Mountains of southern and central Europe. Not British.
Flowering-time July to October.
Description There is something attractively impudent about the way in which these spiny plants settle themselves flat to the ground with outspread leaves so uncomfortable to the unwary traveller seeking rest! Each large silver-sheened inflorescence sits centrally in a prickly patterned circle of leaves, reaching out against competition for ground and sunlight.

In full flower the inflorescence measures from 5 to 13 cm (2 to 5 in) across, the glistening parchment-like ring of bracts being the most conspicuous constituent. Many small tubular florets cover the central receptacle, varying from white through yellow to brown according to age. After pollination, masses of silky-plumed seeds are dispersed by the wind.
Points of Interest Known as the Fair Weather Thistle because the persistent bracts are hygroscopic, these fascinating flower-heads are frequently displayed on outside walls of houses as home weather-forecasters. When growing the bracts are outspread in dry weather and attract pollinating bees; in damp conditions they fold over the flowers to protect them.

The solid receptacle is reputedly edible and the plants also possess stimulant properties.

The name *Carlina* commemorates Charlemagne who, according to legend, used this plant 1200 years ago to cure his soldiers of the plague.

134

Orange Lily *Lilium bulbiferum*
Family: Liliaceae

Habitat Rocky sun-baked slopes and grassland, usually calcareous to 2400 m (8000 ft).
Distribution Pyrenees, Alps, Apennines, Jura, Corsica. Not common. Not British. Strongly protected in France, Italy and Switzerland.
Flowering-time June, July.
Description Flaming torches, burning steadily erect amongst the grey-green backcloth of the steep mountainside, the scattered plants of the Orange or Fire Lily are striking and unmistakable. No other alpine plant possesses flowers so large, so brilliant or so glowing.

Each deeply buried bulb produces one strong erect flowering-stem with numerous narrow leaves about 6 cm ($2\frac{1}{2}$ in) long. There are from one to 5 shortly-stalked upright flowers, widely trumpet-shaped but not tubular. Bright orange outside, the 6 separate petals are yellow-centred inside patterned with small red streaks. Six stamens with orange filaments produce yellow-orange pollen, and the stout style of the same colour arises from a green ovary.
Points of Interest In spite of this wonderful fantasy of colour there seems little evidence of insect-visiting, cross or self-pollination, and rarely the production of seed.

Instead the plants sometimes produce bulbils in the leaf-axils, little dark growths with the power of reproducing new plants without fertilisation. This device is adopted by some mountain plants where conditions are exceptionally unfavourable for growth, pollination, fertilisation and seed production in the short summer experienced by them.

Alpine Hawkweed *Hieracium alpinum* (aggregate)
Family: Compositae

Habitat Alpine and subalpine. Rocky places, cliff ledges, chiefly non-calcareous; 800 to 3000 m (2500 to 10,000 ft).

Distribution The Highlands of Scotland, North Wales and mountains of central and northern Europe.

Flowering-time July and August.

Description Throughout the summer the vivid golden-yellow flowers of Hawkweeds brighten the path of the countryside wanderer in lowlands and uplands alike. But, the large complicated genus provides one of the most difficult taxonomic problems for those who seek to identify the species. Therefore our description of *H. alpinum* (aggregate) is a wide general one fitting the plants in our photograph and leaving details of other sub-species for the would-be specialist to discover for himself.

The plants of the group *alpinum* are confined to hills and mountains where they frequently provide a wonderfully bright display by stony tracks or beckon cheerily – even cheekily – from inaccessible cliff ledges. They light up the gloom of steep clefts and gullies with living candles and they spangle the grass below with gold – gold enhanced with shining silver. Their stems, leaves and bracts are so thickly covered with soft white hairs that they catch and hold the sunlight like fine gossamer.

A challenge to the taxonomist they may be, but none can deny their glorious beauty.

The perennial plants are short, from 8 to 20 cm (3 to 8 in) with erect hairy stems on which grow 2 or 3 small sessile leaves. The larger leaves form a basal rosette; they are about 6 cm ($2\frac{1}{2}$ in) long, slightly toothed and very hairy, the blade narrowing into the stalk.

There is usually one inflorescence about 3 cm ($1\frac{1}{4}$ in) across, a massed head of individual florets surrounded by numerous narrow pointed bracts. These are blackish-green and cloaked by a dense but beautiful covering of white woolly hairs. Each floret is strap-shaped above and tubular below; there are 5 stamens whose united anthers surround the style which divides into 2 curving stigmas. The seeds are small and hard, each with its own cluster or pappus of white hairs which replace the normal calyx in Compositae and which act as parachutes in the dispersal of the seeds by wind.

Points of Interest The name *Hieracium* is derived from the Greek for hawk because it was thought that this sharp-eyed bird extracted the plants' juices to strengthen its sight, even treating the eyes of its young ones. The herbalist Culpeper writing in 1653 includes its application for diseases of human eyes amongst numerous virtues, so perhaps the old legend is not without foundation!

St Bruno's Lily *Paradisea liliastrum*
Family: Liliaceae

Habitat Alpine and subalpine meadows and rocky places often on very steep slopes. From 900 to 2500 m (3000 to 8000 ft).

Distribution Pyrenees, Alps, northern and central Apennines. Very local, but sometimes in good numbers. Protected in Switzerland and France. Not British.

Flowering-time June to August.

Description Though far from traditionally alpine in appearance, these delightful lilies are amongst the most beautiful, most prized and therefore most needful of protection of all alpine plants. Growing as they do in unexpectedly wild places they convert almost inaccessible grim stony hillsides into living white cascades of beauty, so that the sharp contrast thus provided is a sight truly fantastic. The large white flowers appear far too fragile to survive the searing winds, hail and cold swirling mist so frequent in these situations and yet there the lilies grow, emerging from each climatic onslaught as ethereally lovely as ever.

Each member of the colony is distinct with a single erect smooth stem, 20 to 50 cm (8 to 20 in) tall, and a few grasslike leaves of similar length arising from the perennial rootstock. On the stem grow from 2 to 5 large sweet-scented flowers held more or less horizontally on short stalks and which open from the lowest upwards. Each flower is subtended by an erect yellow-green bract twice the length of the stalk and which tapers to a fine point. The white corolla, 5 cm (2 in) long, is composed of 6 petals narrow at the base and widening into a spreading trumpet. Inside the flower 6 stamens grow from the base, with long slender filaments attached to flexible yellow anthers in the mouth of the corolla. The stamens surround a green ovary, grooved and oval, and from which emerges a long style which protrudes beyond the petals when the 3 stigmas are ready for pollination, effected by night-flying moths.

Points of Interest *Paradisea* can be distinguished from the similar *Anthericum liliago* (St Bernard's Lily) by the latter's smaller and more numerous flowers, to about 15 in number and with petals outspread, not forming a trumpet.

The name *Paradisea* was given to this plant by an Italian botanist, Giovanni Mazzucato in honour of his benefactor Count G Paradisi.

The links with St Bruno and St Bernard are more obscure. Both lived in the mountains; St Bruno, the founder of the Carthusian Order of monks, built his first monastery at Chartreuse in France. St Bernard was responsible for the Hospice at the top of the Swiss/Italian Pass which bears his name, and commemorates his care for alpine travellers when travelling was grim. But he, at least, would see *P. liliastrum* adorning the craggy slopes of the pass as it still does so beautifully to this day.

Martagon Lily *Lilium martagon*
Family: Liliaceae

Habitat Grassy slopes and pastures, light woodland, usually calcareous.

Distribution Rare and local in Britain and believed native in parts of southern England, naturalised elsewhere. Not in Ireland but widespread in Europe except in the North. Mostly in the mountains to 2650 m (8000 ft).

Flowering-time June to August.

Description 'If you have two loaves, sell one and buy a lily' says the Eastern proverb. The difficulty would be in the choice of lily for there are so many and all with such a high claim to beauty. The martagons are elegantly beautiful, majestic and dignified; even high on a stony hillside they remain calm and aloof despite the wild winds and wetness which belong to their territory. And when backed by the blue of a summer sky their tall graceful sceptres of curled pink flowers provide a mountain attraction of floral sculpture, which is both exquisite and unusual.

These lilies grow from bulbs each producing one strong smooth erect stem from 30 to 90 cm (1 to 3 ft) tall. Concentric whorls of leaves about 8 cm (3 in) long and from 8 to 12 in number encircle the stem at intervals, an unusual feature.

The inflorescence consists of about 12 flowers (though occasionally there may be 3 times that number) which are perfumed, drooping on fairly long stalks and subtended by leaflike bracts 3 cm ($1\frac{1}{4}$ in) long. Earlier, the tight buds were enclosed in a beautiful thick cocoon of cobwebbed filament which disappeared as the buds unfolded, the lowest ones first. As the flowers develop the dark-spotted pink or reddish petals – rarely white – curl backwards to form the Turk's cap of the plant's popular name.

As with all lilies there are 6 petals and 6 stamens, these latter having long filaments attached to the middle of the large mobile anthers whose orange-red pollen enhances the already attractive colouring. A sturdy style carries a knobby 3-lobed stigma which ripens later. Pollination is carried out by slender-tongued moths which are guided to the nectar at the flower's base by a narrow furrow along the centre of each petal.

Points of Interest The word *martagon* originates from the Turkish name of a special form of turban worn by Sultan Muhammed I and which the reflexed flowers of this lily are supposed to resemble.

The bulbs are dark yellow in colour, a factor which inspired alchemists of old with the hope of making gold from them, a dream which did not materialise! In modern times the flowering plants are a tempting attraction for their regal beauty and, like others already described, their colonies have been much reduced by picking and uprooting. They are now given legal protection in many countries, including Switzerland, France, Germany, Austria and Italy.

Elder-flowered Orchid *Dactylorhiza sambucina*
Family: Orchidaceae

Habitat Mountain grassland, from 500 to 2000 m (1500 to 6000 ft).

Distribution Most European mountains from central Scandinavia southwards, sometimes in large numbers. Not British.

Flowering-time May to July.

Description Yellow is an unusual colour for European orchids and it is therefore all the more exciting to find a mountain pasture or grassy hillside thickly spangled with the compact spikes of this gay little member of that family. When the fresh clear yellow is offset by an intermittent sprinkling of dark pink blooms, as frequently occurs, both the beauty of the scene and the excitement of discovery are enormously enhanced.

From the tuberous rootstock the smooth erect flowering stems attain a height of 10 to 30 cm (4 to 12 in) and carry 5 or 6 large leaves. These are light green, shiny and unspotted about 8 cm (3 in) long, fairly broad and with bases sheathing the stem.

About 10 to 20 flowers pack the short inflorescence, each flower with a long subtending bract. Two narrow petals are curved above the pollinia and the 3 outer sepals, all coloured, are wider and outspread. The lip is fairly large, broader than long and slightly pointed in the centre and behind is a long conical downward pointing spur.

The above description applies to both colour forms but there are small variations in colour and pattern. The lip of the yellow flowers is usually lightly decorated with purple or reddish spots, and the bracts are pale green. The pink and purple-red flowers may have a pale patch near the top of the lip and also red-tinted bracts.

Points of Interest There are four other species of yellow-flowered European orchids, all rather similar to each other and to our plant. Only one, *Orchis pallens* Pale-flowered Orchid, is also a mountain plant of central Europe which lessens the problem of identification. The position of the flower-spurs is a useful guide as those of *O. pallens* are either horizontal or, more often pointing upward, while those of *D. sambucina* are directed downward. *O. pallens* flowers possess a rather deeply 3-lobed lip, quite different in outline from the wide one of our description above.

Confusion does arise with the specific epithet *sambucina*. This is derived from *Sambucus* the generic name for the well-known Elderberry bush with its masses of heavily sweet-scented flowers. *D. sambucina* has little if any perfume. *Orchis pallens* is the plant with a scent reminiscent of the Elderberry flowers.

The remaining three yellow orchids *Dactylorhiza romana*, *Orchis provincialis* and its subspecies *pauciflora* grace the Mediterranean region in rather local beautiful colonies.

Black Vanilla Orchid   *Nigritella nigra*
Family: Orchidaceae

Habitat Alpine and subalpine meadows and grassy places.
Distribution All European mountains from the Pyrenees to the Carpathians, also Scandinavia. From 1000 to 2800 m (3300 to 9000 ft) and locally frequent. Not British.
Flowering-time June to August.
Description Where the green turf is short on boulder-strewn mountain slopes the quaint little wine-red heads of the Vanilla Orchid are easily singled out from other vegetation because their colour is unique amongst the alpine flora. Despite the names *nigra* and 'black', the flowers are not quite so dark, but the unopened buds are so near that colour that from a distance black is one's first impression. The brighter yellows, blues and whites of their immediate neighbours emphasise rather than hide the small round dark knobs of flowers. Although local, it may sometimes be found in quantity when the plants are scattered liberally over the rough ground.

The plants are variable in size from as short as 5 cm (2 in) to an occasional 25 cm (10 in) but usually about 10 cm (4 in). Stems and leaves are yellow-green, the stems slightly furrowed and the numerous narrow grasslike leaves are spirally arranged and sheathing at the base.

The tiny buds are packed into a dense conical head which becomes globular as the flowers emerge, often as many as 50. Though so small and tightly wedged their spiral arrangement gives each one adequate space and light, an excellent example of the ensurance of these important factors. The buds open from the base upwards and the vanilla-scented flowers on close inspection have the appearance of 6-pointed stars. They are sessile, subtended by light green leaflike bracts, red-tipped, and longer than the ovary. Of the 6 petals the uppermost is the largest and is pointed and slightly folded. This is really the lip or labellum which in most European orchids is at the base of the flower, hanging downwards. The remaining 5 petals are outspread and narrow and the tiny blunt spur is shorter than the straight green ovary.
Points of Interest This, probably the best-loved of alpine orchids, is a fascinating subject for legends. One tells of a monk who spent many days in prayer before a statue of the Christchild in a cathedral. He was overcome by the desire to possess part of the statue and, breaking off an arm, fled with it into the mountains. However, retribution followed and he became completely lost, and on the point of dying he buried the arm nearby. The following year, on the ledge where his body was found grew the dark red flowers of this sweetly-scented beautiful little orchid – whose small palmately divided tubers resemble the shape of a child's hand.

Deservedly so, it is protected at least in Austria, Bavaria, France and Switzerland.

Feather Grass *Stipa pennata*
Family: Graminae

Habitat Dry stony grassland, to 2500 m (8000 ft).
Distribution Most of central and south east Europe. Not British.
Flowering-time May to July.
Description Most plants delight us with their colours, enhanced by the overall greenery of surrounding vegetation, flowerless like mosses or insignificantly flowered as in the vast kingdom of grasses – the family *Graminae*. But a few exceptions to these inconspicuous plants erupt at flowering-time into a sea of beauty which needs no adornment; such an exception is *Stipa pennata*, the waving Feather Grass of stony hillsides. What a superb picture we have when low evening sunlight transforms myriads of windblown feathers into long streamers of shining silver, as in our first photograph. Alternatively scattered groups of plants share bouldery mountain slopes with red dianthus, blue campanulas and pink sleepy sempervivums when a hot summer breeze gently wafts the soft silky plumes of *Stipa*.

The plants are perennial and densely tufted with several narrow glaucous green leaves, pointed and with inrolled margins. As usual in grasses, the lower part forms a sheath round the stem, a protective device in early growth. Each flower-head is composed of a few yellowish-green spikelets enclosing tiny flowers which possess neither sepals nor petals, only stamens and pistils. This is the usual flower form in the grass family.

But not all grasses can display the attractive appearance of the feathery plumes or awns of *Stipa* which are really a wonderful mechanism of great practical value; a device to aid the dispersal of the seeds. Each seed is sharply pointed with a tuft of backwardly directed hairs behind the point. Behind the seed (17 mm long), the awn is spirally twisted for about 6 cm (2½ in) before the plume, some 20 to 30 cm (8 to 12 in) long takes over. This is clothed with beautifully soft short white hairs, and when the seeds are ripe, the whole plume breaks away from the stem and takes to the air like an arrow. When it eventually falls to the ground the seed-point penetrates the soil and is driven deeper by the corkscrew twisting of the spiral in hygroscopic response to the humidity of the atmosphere.

Points of Interest Although its fascinating method of seed dispersal is the most interesting fact about this unusual grass, it is not the only one. The plants have no need of attractively coloured flowers because, like almost all grasses, they depend upon the wind for pollination, the pollen being light and blown from one plant to another. These two factors together must be of great assistance to plants in places where winds are usually strong, and windless days extremely rare. The production of large quantities of pollen and seeds in these circumstances will ensure their best chance of survival with the aid of these beautifully appointed modifications.

Trailing Azalea *Loiseleuria procumbens*
Family: Ericaceae

Habitat Arctic-alpine. Dry stony places of exposed mountain moors on acid soil.

Distribution Pyrenees, Alps and Carpathians at 1500 to 3000 m (5000 to 10,000 ft). Arctic, north west Scotland to 1200 m (nearly 4000 ft).

Flowering-time Between June and August.

Description High moors and mountain plateaux exposed to the coldest strongest winds, above the sheltering alpine tree-line or gripped in the icily low temperatures of the arctic north, appear most unsuitable for plant-life. However, there the ground-hugging stems and leathery leaves of the Trailing Azalea cover acres of stony windswept ground, their low-growing habit being a perfect adaptation to such bleak conditions. During the short summer the whole area undergoes an incredible transformation when thousands of starry flowers shed a pink glow over the boulders, often sharing them with lichens as in our photograph.

Each plant, scarcely 10 cm (4 in) above ground, is much branched and densely packed with small evergreen leaves which are dark green above with margins recurved to control loss of water. The flowers possess 5 red sepals, a 5-petalled pink corolla, 5 stamens with red anthers and one pistil.

Points of Interest Named after the French botanist J. L. A. Loiseleur-Deslongchamps.

How tough and long-lived are these beautiful plants of the high mountains. The Swiss botanist Professor Carl Schroeter counted 55 annual rings in the 'trunk' of one plant – each ring less than 0.1 mm in width – representing 55 years of slow but steady growth!

Purple Saxifrage *Saxifraga oppositifolia*
Family: Saxifragaceae

Habitat Arctic-alpine. Wet rocks, screes, glacier moraines, from sea-level (Scotland, Norway, Greenland and Spitzbergen), to 3800 m (12,450 ft) in the Alps.

Distribution From arctic Europe, south through most mountain ranges (including the British Isles) to the Sierra Nevada (Spain).

Flowering-time Between April and August, depending upon altitude and latitude.

Description What wonderful plants these are! Large purple flowers cascade in living beauty down mountain gullies and by rocky streams; they decorate the loose stones of morainic debris with brilliant colour; they drape sea cliffs and alpine ledges with curtains patterned with mingled leaves and blossoms; and all amid scenes of snow-decked grandeur.

Creeping, trailing or hanging, the wiry branching stems often reach 30 cm (1 ft) in length, and are clothed with numerous pairs of tiny dark green leaves, their margins fringed with hairs. The comparatively large flowers, 10 to 15 mm (about $\frac{1}{2}$ in) across, are variable in colour from pale pink to rich purple with 5 spreading rounded petals and 5 tiny sepals. Ten stamens surround the ovary with its 2 styles and stigmas. The fruits are dry brown capsules often persisting after seed dispersal.

Points of Interest Remarkable for its wide geographical and altitudinal range throughout the Northern Hemisphere. From America's Rocky Mountains, Alaska and Greenland, via Spitzbergen and Europe it crosses northern Asia. It grows in the most northerly plant locality at 83° 15′ N on Greenland. A survivor from the Ice Age and a wonderful plant!

Yellow Alpine Poppy *Papaver rhaeticum*
Family: Papaveraceae

Habitat Alpine screes, moraines, debris, stony river beds, between 1800 and 3000 m (6000 and 10,000 ft). Occasionally carried lower by streams to 1200 m (4000 ft). Likes limestone.

Distribution Endemic to Europe. South west and eastern Alps, eastern Pyrenees; very local. Not British.

Flowering-time July and August.

Description High up in the mountains where retreating glaciers have piled up stones and rocks, these tenacious and enchanting alpine poppies brighten the vast gaunt wilderness with splashes of brilliant gold in defiance of the everlasting wind.

A strong perennial rootstock helps to keep these vivid plants anchored among the shifting stones, and from these arise thin bristly-haired stems 6 to 20 cm ($2\frac{1}{2}$ to 8 in) tall. All leaves are basal, dark green and unevenly lobed. The solitary 4-petalled flowers measure from 3 to 4 cm ($1\frac{1}{4}$ to $1\frac{1}{2}$ in) across, and unfold delicately between 2 dark hairy sepals which soon fall away. Numerous stamens and a 5-rayed ovary fill the centre of the flowers, and eventually dry seeds fill the typical poppy capsules ready for wind dispersal.

Points of Interest These small seeds are shaken from the capsule's ring of holes by the wind into crevices between loose stones. During winter storms or with the spring-melting snow some of them are washed down the mountainside to reach security again on shingly river banks at lower altitudes – as low as 1200 m (4000 ft) and there new colonies are formed.

Papaver sendtneri, a white-flowered species, replaces *P. rhaeticum* on limestone.

150

Bear's-ear *Primula auricula*
Family: Primulaceae

Habitat Alpine and subalpine. Cliff faces, gullies and crevices, stony grassland, on limestone; from about 800 to 2750 m (2600 to 9000 ft).
Distribution Endemic to Europe. Widespread but local and uncommon through the Alps, Carpathians and Apennines. Not British.
Flowering-time June, July.
Description 'The Glory of the Alps' and the 'Precipice Flower' are remarkably descriptive names which fit the brilliant Auriculas perfectly. They glow high in narrow clefts and chinks like scattered lamps in a dark corridor. They bejewel steep wild cliffs with pendants of shining gold, and like gold they are usually difficult to reach.

Sturdy but flexible stems up to 8 cm (3 in) grow singly within a circle of grey-green leaves, thick and rounded-oval, the Bear's ears of its popular name. Their slightly crenate margins are whitish and cartilaginous which with the leathery texture restricts loss of water. Each stem carries an umbel of from 2 to 12 large sweet-scented flowers of typical *Primula* structure. Calyx and corolla are tubular, the petals notched at the apex and the position of 5 stamens and single pistil either 'thrum' or 'pin-eyed' to ensure cross-pollination (see *P. scotica* page 11). A white mealy deposit encircles the throat of the corolla.
Points of Interest Like the Edelweiss it has been so ravaged in its lower haunts where it thrived on richer soil. Let us hope that its lawful protection will mean that these plants of beauty remain 'a joy for ever'.

151

Moss Campion *Silene acaulis*
Family: Caryophyllaceae

Habitat Arctic-alpine, on rocks, stony grassland, mountain and sea-cliffs, usually calcareous.

Distribution Fairly frequent in Scotland on mountains from 750 to 1220 m (2500 to 3600 ft) and on coastal cliffs in the north-west. Rare in the English Lake District and North Wales; very rare in Ireland. Widespread and common in the Alps, Pyrenees, Apennines and Carpathians, from 1500 to 3500 m (5000 to 12,000 ft), and in arctic Europe from the lowlands to 2000 m (6500 ft).

Flowering-time June to August depending on altitude and situation.

Description Of all mountain-plants Moss Campion provides one of the most enchantingly vivid displays of rich colour in the summer months. It is a cushion-plant and the rocky pastures of the Alps are bedecked with large brilliant hummocks of glowing pink, nestling against grey boulders and often with white flowers of *Dryas octopetala* (Mountain Avens) nearby. On steep cliffs it forms beautiful cascades as in the photograph, a mode of growth frequently seen in its British situations.

This luxuriant display of flowers cloaks a plant of wonderful construction and adaptation to its inhospitable surroundings and fierce weather. Each cushion possesses a tap-root of great tenacity which anchors it firmly in its stony home withstanding many a storm and upheaval. Indeed plants can sometimes be seen literally 'hanging by the roots', when adverse conditions have resulted in the erosion of their terrain.

The cushion base is composed of short stems and densely packed bright green mosslike leaves. During the flowering season these leaves may be completely hidden by the rosy pink flowers, one to a stem, and each 10 to 15 mm (about $\frac{1}{2}$ in) across. There are 5 petals slightly notched, and spreading wide above a narrow tube, the flowers being pollinated by butterflies. Their long tongues can penetrate the flower-tube to reach the nectar at its base, but crawling insects are debarred by the presence of a tiny scale at the base of each petal. Cross-pollination between plants is effectively ensured as stamens and pistils are mostly produced on separate plants. Where flowers possess both these sets of organs they ripen separately, but here self-pollination is possible, a safeguard in case of a shortage of butterflies in a bad season.

The small seeds develop in dry brown capsules from which they are blown by the wind which scatters them in all directions before the early frost and snows of winter descend upon the land.

Edelweiss *Leontopodium alpinum*
Family: Compositae

Habitat Alpine meadows, rocks and stony places, preferring limestone, from about 2000 to 3000 m (7000 to 10,000 ft).

Distribution Through the mountains of central and south east Europe into Asia and Siberia. Protected throughout the Alps. Not British.

Flowering-time July and August.

Description Edelweiss is more surrounded by a halo of romance, horrifying tales of neck-breaking climbs, and commercial exploitation than any other plant of the mountains of Europe. But, so long as all this can be kept in perspective these furry-felted little plants can be enjoyed and appreciated for what they really are – mountain gems.

Their geographical range is extremely wide, from the Pyrenees and Alps across Europe and Asia through the Himalayas to Siberia. Although they do grow on dangerous cliffs they once were plentiful on stony grassland until they were collected almost to extinction in such accessible places.

What is the plant's strong attraction, for visitors to the Alps especially? Those people who have seen it only in cultivation can have little idea of its charm in the wild. There the plants are short, no taller than they need be to hold up their flower-heads to the light and the spreading felted stars with feathery yellow centres are exquisitely formed. They are almost everlasting and their mountain surroundings, permanently snow-capped, are wonderfully wild and exciting.

In such places the perennial stems are only 5 to 10 cm (2 to 4 in) tall with a few small leaves. The larger leaves are all basal, their green colour just visible beneath the exceptionally thick cloak of white hairs. The attractively pointed flower-star consists of about 8 bracts, so densely hairy that the rarely-used English name Flannel flower is truly applicable, though perhaps unimpressive. Within the circle of bracts is a tight cluster of from 5 to 10 small inflorescences each composed of several tiny florets. At first these are off-white in colour like the rest of the plant but as they mature little brushes of golden stamens are thrust out on top, from the central inflorescence first, the encircling ones later. The first stage is portrayed in our July photograph.

Points of Interest High-growing alpine plants are frequently hairy; we have already seen that in *Pulsatilla* and *Hieracium*, but the dense covering of Edelweiss is the most obvious of them all. The chief function of the hairs in all such plants is to reduce evaporation of water and prevent the plants from drying out in such difficult climatic conditions. Edelweiss is believed to have reached Europe from Siberia during the Ice Ages and its natural furry coat has proved eminently suitable for European mountain situations. In this plant also the felted starry bracts assume the task of normal coloured petals, the attraction for pollinating insects.

Snowdon Lily *Lloydia serotina*
Family: Liliaceae

Habitat Stony grassland, cliff ledges and gullies in mountains, to 900 m (3000 ft) in Wales, and to 3000 m (10,000 ft) in Europe.

Distribution The mountains of North Wales only in Britain. Very rare and protected by law. In Europe, from the Alps to the Caucasus, Arctic Russia, the Urals.

Flowering-time June, July.

Description Snowdon Lily is a charming plant with no grandeur or brilliance, simply a tiny unspoilt beauty which no cultivated elegance can surpass. Its pale flowers bespangle rocky grassland, though sparingly, and the plants cling to grass-covered ledges of overhanging cliffs where torrents and waterfalls tear gashes in the steep mountainside. There its numbers are few and scattered, but how the grim background suits them! Here is a first-class example of that amazing contrast between the grandeur of magnificent scenery and the frail daintiness of exquisite little plants which can be experienced only among the mountains.

Lloydia serotina is one of the few really high-growing plants in Europe which over-winters by means of a bulb. Bulbous plants are associated with warm or hot countries for frozen ground does not suit them, but this small species is an exception to that rule. The reddish stems are only from 5 to 15 cm (2 to 6 in) tall and carry 3 or 4 short leaves, while a few longer grasslike ones emerge from the base. The flowers are usually single (occasionally 2), cup-shaped at first and white etched with delicate lines of yellow and brownish-red. Sepals and petals are alike, 6 altogether, oval and spreading out as the 6 stamens, and later the stigma, mature. Small nectaries within the base of the flower attract flies for pollination even at high altitudes.

Points of Interest A Welsh botanist, Edward Llwyd discovered this plant in Snowdonia in 1688 but it was not until after his death in 1709 that it was named in his honour.

The worldwide distribution is extremely exciting for such frail-looking plants, for they are found all round the northern hemisphere, from western North America across Europe into Asia, north to arctic Russia and through the Himalayas to China and Japan. But perhaps the most puzzling colony is still that small one in Wales 1050 km (700 miles) from its nearest neighbours in the Alps and 7500 km (5000 miles) from those in North America. It is now one of the U.K.'s legally protected plants; we have in the past lost so much of it by collecting that we must definitely keep what is left, not only for its beauty and British interest, but because of its peculiar world position – an important stepping-stone, between the Old and the New Worlds.

As with the local endemic plants, we must in all countries remember in our Plant Protection Laws those like *Lloydia serotina* whose world distribution justifies the need for especial care for small colonies which have their place in the fascinating uncompleted jigsaw of worldwide ecology.

Alpine Androsace *Androsace alpina*
Family: Primulaceae

Habitat High alpine. Moraines, debris, screes, gravel, on primary rocks, from 2000 to 4200 m (7000 to just below 14,000 ft). It is recorded at 4200 m on the Matterhorn, only 300 m (1000 ft) below the summit.

Distribution Endemic to the European Alps; Austria, France, Italy, Switzerland (where protected). Not British.

Flowering-time July, August.

Description *Androsace alpina* is a jewel of a plant; always at high altitudes, never frequent, often inaccessible, infinitely beautiful and a rare delight.

Its rockbound homes are surrounded by the highest peaks of the alpine range, permanently blanketed with deep snow. Here even in summer frost is not unknown, winds blow strong and cold, and chilling mist or violent storms alternate with the mountain brilliance of sun and sky.

In such harsh conditions these plants produce rock-hugging cushions of exquisite rose or shell-pink flowers which bring startling life to a scene otherwise bleak indeed. Neither are they alone; nearby may be found blue stars of *Eritrichium nanum*, creamy saxifrages, vivid purple and orange *Linaria alpina* (toadflax) and purple primulas – and more! Even so the view holds far more stones than flowers, much more snow than rock.

These plants therefore are all individuals of great tenacity, life and beauty, each one more than worthy of the magnificent grandeur of its setting.

King of the Alps *Eritrichium nanum*
Family: Boraginaceae

Habitat High alpine, on rock faces, clefts, scree, usually granite, 2500 to 3600 m (8000 to 11,800 ft).

Distribution Local in the European Alps, rare and protected. Not British.

Flowering-time July, August.

Description and Points of Interest For some eight months of the year deep snow covers the home of these exquisite plants. Only when this melts from warm south-facing cliffs do cushions of silvery-haired leaves appear, supported by long woody roots, which pentrate all available cracks for nutriment. As the sun strengthens, the leaves are hidden by close-packed flowers of enchanting blue (rarely white), and the King of the Alps – Herald of Heaven – call it what you will – reigns supreme for another brief season of sheer beauty.

Lichens are its neighbours, extraordinary flowerless plants which pattern the rocks with tawny yellows and reds. Insignificant they may appear, but how important they are. Their minute wind-dispersed spores settle in narrow cracks to produce small plants which on dying form pockets of humus. This is a continuing process over the years until sufficient humus accumulates to provide larger flowering plants with a roothold and food.

Then can *Eritrichium*, *Androsace* and their kind emerge in matchless beauty, their brilliant flowers outshining but not deposing the unspectacular lichens. Each has equal value in the kingdom of mountain plants.

159

Glacier Crowfoot *Ranunculus glacialis*
Family: Ranunculaceae

Habitat Arctic-alpine. Primary rocks, mountains 2300 to 4275 m (7500 to 14,000 ft).
Distribution Arctic Europe, central European mountains. Not British.
Flowering-time July, August.
Description Only the wildest places of the highest mountains are blessed with the abundant beauty of these two plants frequently found together. Both appear to defy all the laws of the mountain flora – no compact cushions for them, no thick coat of hairs or reduced leaves. Instead a glorious abandon of large cheerful wide-open flowers flinging defiance against the worst the weather can do. We have reached the most wonderful rock-garden of all.

Glacier Crowfoot usually grows in clusters with glossy stems to 15 cm (6 in) and lobed leaves typical of the genus. The flowers are 3 cm ($1\frac{1}{4}$ in) across, white when young gradually changing to rosy pink reputedly after pollination – by insects despite the altitude. The 5 sepals are a distinguishing character; they are brownish red with hairs and are persistent.
Points of Interest Our photograph depicts a typical group of the Glacier Crowfoot at 3000 m (10,000 ft) with *Geum reptans* behind it; above this, the Crowfoot becomes almost stemless, with hairy leaves. At 4275 m (14,100 ft) on the Swiss Finsteraarhorn, the crowfoots are the highest-growing flowering plants in Europe. So here on these timeless heights we leave them:

> 'On a throne of rocks, in a robe of clouds.
> With a diadem of snow.'   Lord Byron

Glossary

ACUMINATE Narrowing gradually to a point; of leaf, sepal, etc.

ANNUAL A plant which grows, sets seed and withers within 12 months.

ANNUAL RING Circular mark in cross-section of tree trunk indicating one year's growth.

ANTHER Upper part of stamen which contains pollen.

AURICLE Small ear-like projection at base of leaf.

AWN Stiff bristle-like projection in grass flowers.

AXIL Angle between a leaf or bract and the stem.

BIENNIAL A plant which completes its life-cycle within two years, flowering in the second year.

BIFID Divided deeply into two parts.

BRACT Small leaf-like structure, from the axil of which a flower often grows.

CALCICOLE A plant usually growing on chalk or lime-based soil.

CALYX The sepals as a whole, whether free or united.

CAPSULE A dry fruit, which usually splits to release the seeds.

CARPEL A single section of the ovary or fruit.

CARTILAGINOUS Tough and hard, like cartilage.

COLUMN Structure in the centre of an orchid flower; formed by the fusion of stamens, style and stigma.

COROLLA The petals as a whole, whether free or united.

CRENATE Of leaf-margins with rounded teeth.

ENDEMIC Native of, and confined to, a specific region.

FIBROUS Thin and thread-like, as of some roots.

FILAMENT The stalk of the stamen which carries the anther.

FLORET A small flower, usually one of a dense cluster as in the family Compositae.

GARIGUE Mediterranean vegetation characterised by low shrubs less than 1 m (39 in) tall on dry areas, often between the coast and the maquis.

GLABROUS Smooth, without hairs.

GLAND Organ of secretion, often on tip of hairs.

GLAUCOUS Covered with bloom, bluish.

INFLORESCENCE The complete flowering section of a stem; a collection of individual flowers together, e.g. daisy, orchid, foxglove.

LABELLUM Lip; a modified petal, or fused petals, distinct from other petals especially in orchids and the families Labiatae and Scrophulariaceae.

MAQUIS Thickets of shrubs, 2 m (78 in) or more tall, often dense, with scattered trees; characteristic of the Mediterranean region.

NECTAR Sweet substance produced by plants to attract insects.

OVARY The lowest part of the pistil, enclosing ovules.

OVULE Small egg-like structure, which develops into a seed after fertilisation.

PALMATE Divided in a hand-like way, usually of leaves.

PANICLE A type of inflorescence branched and spreading, e.g. Sea-kale and some grasses.

PERENNIAL A plant which lives for more than two years, usually flowering each year.

PERFECT Of a flower; one possessing both stamens and pistil.

PERIANTH Floral leaves as a whole, whether distinct sepals and petals, e.g. buttercups or all similar and coloured, e.g. lilies.

PETAL One of the inner ring of floral leaves, usually though not always, large and coloured.

PINNATE The arrangement of leaflets in two rows.

PISTIL The flower's female reproductive organ composed of stigma, style and ovary.

POLLEN Small grains which contain the male reproductive cells.

POLLINATION The transference of pollen from the stamens to a stigma; in cross-pollination, to the stigma of a different flower.

POLLINIA A structure formed from a mass of pollen-grains in orchid flowers.

PROBOSCIS Elongated mouth-part of some insects.

RACEME Long inflorescence with stalked flowers.

REVOLUTE Rolled downwards or onto the underside (of leaves).

RHIZOME Perennial underground stem.

SEPAL One of the outer ring of floral leaves, typically green but not always.

SESSILE Without a stalk.

SHEATH The base of a leaf enveloping the stem.

SPATHULATE Spoon-shaped; like a spatula – of leaves.

SPIKELET One or more florets in a group; of grass flowers.

SPUR Hollow tubular extension of a flower often containing nectar.

STAMEN One of the male reproductive organs of a flower.

STIGMA The receptive surface of the pistil to which pollen adheres.

STYLE The stalk-like connection between the ovary and stigma.

SUBTEND The way in which a bract or leaf encloses a flower between itself and the stem.

TAPROOT A solid, descending main root.

TAXONOMY The classification of plants and animals in systematic order.

TERRESTRIAL Plants growing in the ground, i.e. the majority of European flowering-plants.

TUBER A swollen part of the stem or root, formed annually and usually underground; stores food.

UMBEL An inflorescence in which the flower-stalks arise together from the top of the main stem, like an umbrella, as in the family Umbelliferae.

Bibliography and Further Reading

Blunt, Wilfred *The Compleat Naturalist* (*A Life of Linnaeus*) Collins, London, 1971.

Clair, Colin *Of Herbs and Spices* Abelard-Schuman, London, 1961.

Clapham, A. R., Tutin, T. G. and Warburg, E. F. *Flora of the British Isles* University Press, Cambridge, 1962.

Culpeper, Nicholas *Complete Herbal* Foulsham, London, 1968.

Fitter, Richard, Fitter, Alastair and Blamey, Marjorie *The Wild Flowers of Britain and Northern Europe* Collins, London, 1974.

Christiansen, M. Skytle *The Pocket Encyclopaedia of Wild Flowers in Colour* Blandford Press, Poole, 1974.

Gerard, John *Leaves from Gerard's Herbal* Thorsons, London, 1972.

Gjaerevoll, Olav and Jørgensen, Reidar *Mountain Flowers of Scandinavia* Trondhjems Turistforening, Trondheim, 1963.

Hegi, Gustav *Alpine Flowers* Blackie, London 1930.

Hepburn, Ian *Flowers of the Coast* Collins, London, 1952.

Heywood, V. H. *et al. Flowering Plants of the World* Oxford University Press, Oxford, 1978.

Holden, Alexander E. *Plant Life in the Scottish Highlands* Oliver and Boyd, Edinburgh, 1952.

Hutchinson, John *British Wild Flowers*, Vols 1 and 2, David and Charles, Newton Abbott, 1972.

Huxley, Anthony and Taylor, William *Flowers of Greece and the Aegean* Chatto and Windus, London, 1977.

Huxley, Anthony *Mountain Flowers in Colour* Blandford Press, Poole, 1967.

Hyde, H. A. and Wade, A. E. *Welsh Flowering Plants* National Museum of Wales, Cardiff, 1957.

Kleijn, H. and Vermeulen, P. *The Beauty of the Wild Plant* Harrap, London, 1964.

Landolt, Elias *Geschützte Pflanzen in der Schweiz* 2nd edn. Schweizerischer Bund fur Naturschutz, Basle, 1975.

Lousley, J. E. *Wild Flowers of Chalk and Limestone* 2nd edn. Collins, London, 1971.

Martin, W. Keble *The Concise British Flora in Colour* Ebury Press and Michael Joseph, London, 1976.

Perring, F. H. and Walters, S. M. (Eds.) *Atlas of the British Flora* 2nd edn. E.P. Publishing (for the Botanical Society of the British Isles), Wakefield, 1976.

Polunin, Oleg *Flowers of Europe* Oxford University Press, Oxford, 1969.

Polunin, Oleg and Huxley, Anthony *Flowers of the Mediterranean* Chatto and Windus, London, 1965.

Polunin, Oleg and Smythies, B. E. *Flowers of South-west Europe* Oxford University Press, 1973.

Praeger, R. Lloyd *The Botanist in Ireland* E.P. Publishing, Wakefield, 1974.

Rarău-Bichiceanu, Rodica and Bichiceanu, Mircea *Flowers of Rumania* Meridiane Publishing House, Bucharest, 1964.

Raven, John and Walters, Max *Mountain Flowers* Collins, London, 1956.

Schroeter, Carl *Alpen-Flora* 27th edn. Raustein Verlag, Zurich.

Summerhayes, V. S. *Wild Orchids of Britain* 2nd edn. Collins, London, 1968.

Taylor, Norman E. and Mathews, F. Schuyler *Field Book of American Wild Flowers* Putnam, New York, 1955.

Thompson, H. Stuart *Alpine Plants of Europe* Routledge, London, 1911.

Thompson, H. Stuart *Subalpine Plants* Routledge, London, 1912.

Thompson, H. Stuart *Flowering Plants of the Riviera* Longmans, Green, London, 1914.

Tosco, Uberto *The World of Mountain Flowers* Orbis, London, 1974.

Tutin, T. G. *et al.* (Eds.) *Flora Europaea* Vols. 1–4 Cambridge University Press, Cambridge, 1976.

Vareschi, Volkmar and Krause, Ernst *Mountains in Flower* Lindsay Drummond, London, 1947.

Williams, John G., Williams, Andrew E. and Arlott, Norman *A Field Guide to the Orchids of Britain and Europe* Collins, London, 1978.

Index of English Names

Page numbers refer to photographs; the descriptive texts are below the photograph (half-page photographs), or on the facing page (full-page photographs).

Index of Latin Names

Page numbers refer to photographs: the descriptive texts are below the photograph (half-page photographs), or on the facing page (full-page photographs).